Liberal Irish, Association Liberal Unionist

The Speaker's handbook on the Irish question

Liberal Irish, Association Liberal Unionist

The Speaker's handbook on the Irish question

ISBN/EAN: 9783744740753

Printed in Europe, USA, Canada, Australia, Japan

Cover: Foto ©Andreas Hilbeck / pixelio.de

THE

SPEAKER'S HAND-BOOK

ON THE

IRISH QUESTION.

BY

AN IRISH LIBERAL.

Third and Enlarged Edition.

PRINTED FOR AND PUBLISHED BY
THE LIBERAL UNIONIST ASSOCIATION,
31, GREAT GEORGE STREET, WESTMINSTER, S.W.

Price 6d., or post free, 9d.

PREFACE TO THIRD EDITION.

THE first two editions having been sold out, it has been thought advisable to issue a third edition at a cheaper price, so as to bring this Hand-book within the reach of politicians of every class. Opportunity has also been taken to add certain passages where the arguments appeared incomplete, and to bring the great Irish controversy in its varying phases down to the most recent date. It is hoped that the book in its present shape will supply all that is needful to rebut the numerous fallacies employed by speakers on the Home Rule side.

A complete list of the publications of the Liberal Unionist Association will be found at pp. 191—198.

December, 1889.

PREFACE.

THE object of this little work is to collect together in a handy form the various lines of argument which go together to make up the Home Rule controversy, and also those facts—legal, historical, and statistical—which ought to form so important a part of all serious discussion on the Irish Question.

That question naturally divides itself into three heads, which therefore suggest the main divisions of this Hand-book. First is the question of HOME RULE itself. Secondly, the law and facts of the LAND QUESTION, which plays so important a part in current controversy. Thirdly, it is obviously a necessity to deal with those topics which are generally alluded to as the incidents of what is called "COERCION."

Some additional information which does not readily fall under these heads is added in Supplemental sections; tables are given in all necessary cases, and it is hoped that, with the aid of a full index, this primer will be of service both to speakers and to inquirers after truth.

December, 1888.

SYNOPSIS.

Part I.

HOME RULE.

DEFINITION.

PAGE

Home Rule not Local Government 1
Mr. John Dillon on Home Rule and Local Government ... 2, 3

ARGUMENTS FOR HOME RULE 3

A. Demanded by Majority of Irish People ... ... 4—15
Unionist Reply 5
Gladstonians do not believe in National Rights of Ireland 6
Ireland a Nation? 6
The Rights of a Nation 6
The Marks of a Nation 7, 8
1. Geographical Position 8
2. Historical Growth 8
3. Distinct Origin 9
Mr. Gladstone on the Irish Race 9
Minorities and Majorities 10
Question of Majorities depends on Area 10
The Loyalists and a Second Parliament 11
The Question of Ulster 12, 13
Ulster Constituencies 13
Ulster Votes in 1886 13
The Constitution of the Irish Majority and Minority 14, 15

B. Misgovernment in the Past ... ... 16—28
Dates of Irish History 16
The Kingdom of Ireland 17
Ireland and Civilisation 17

PAGE

The Early Population of Ireland 17
The English Pale 18
Home Rule Nonsense about Invaders 18
The Old Irish Parliament 19
Poynings' Law 19
Ireland under Elizabeth 20
The Reformation in Ireland 21
The Plantation of Ulster 21
Strafford in Ireland 21
The Great Rebellion 22
Oliver Cromwell 22, 23
Ireland under Charles II. 23
Ireland under James II. 23, 24
The Penal Laws 24
Roman Catholic Disabilities 25
Ireland from 1700 to 1782 25
Grattan's Parliament 26, 27
Imperial Government since the Union 27, 28

C. The Irish People Defrauded in 1800 ... ... 28—33

First Fiction. That the Union was Carried against the consent of the Irish People 29

All the Roman Catholics in favour of the Union 29, 30

Absurd Statement by the Younger Grattan 28

Second Fiction. Bribery and Corruption 31

List of Moneys paid to Men who Voted against the Government ... 32

Creation of Peerages 32

D. Alleged Failure of the Union ... ... 33—39
Lord Clare on Ireland in 1800 ... ... 33, 34
Decline of the Population of Ireland 35
Decline of Population in Agricultural Parts of Great Britain 36
Belfast under the Act of Union 37
Commercial Progress of Ireland 37
The Revenue 37
The Shipping 37
The Excise 38
The Savings Banks 38
The Post Office Savings Banks 38

PAGE

Housing of the People 38
Education 38
National Schools 38
Consent of the Governed 39
Coercion Acts 39

E. That Home Rule has succeeded elsewhere ... 40—43
Home Rule in Europe 40, 41
Home Rule in the Colonies 42
Home Rule in the United States 42

F. Alleged Land Grievances 43

G. Coercion the Alternative to Home Rule 43

Mr. Gladstone's Bill of 1886—Synopsis of ... ... 44—48

Sectarian Endowment 47

The Separatist Objects of Irish Home Rulers ... 48, 49
Sample Utterances :—
Mr. Parnell at Dublin, 1880 48
Mr. Parnell at Cincinnati, 1880 48
Mr. W. Redmond in the House of Commons, 1884 ... 48
Mr. Sexton at Dublin, 1881 48
Mr. W. O'Brien at Gorey, 1885 48
Mr. Parnell at Ennis, 1885 49
Mr. J. Redmond at Chicago, 1886 49

The Union of Hearts 49
Mr. John O'Connor at Ballylooby, 1888 49
Mr. John Dillon at Thurles, 1888 49
Mr. John Dillon at Waterford, 1888 49

Home Rule Impracticable ... ... 50—63
A Scheme of Home Rule 50
Exclusion of the Irish Members 51
Taxation and Representation 53
The North American Colonies 53
Retention of the Irish Members 53
Mr. Gladstone *v.* Mr. Gladstone (on Retention) ... 54, 55
Imperial *v.* Local Affairs 55
Federalism ... ... 58—61
Home Rule Not a Final Settlement ... 61—63

Part II.

THE IRISH LAND QUESTION.

PAGE
Agriculture the Great Irish Industry 64
Agriculture in Ireland mainly Pastoral 65
Small Holdings 65
Rating 65
Extent 65
The Irish Acre 66
Extent of Uncultivated Land 66
The Hanging Gale 66
History of the Irish Land Question 67
The Famine of 1846-47 68
The Land Laws prior to 1870 ... ... 69—71
1. The Poor Relief Acts, 1838-43 69
2. Act for Relief of Destitute Poor, 1848 69
3. Landlord and Tenant Act of 1860 70
Tenants' Improvements 70, 71
Landlord and Tenant Act, 1870 ... ... 72—75
Compensation for Disturbance 73
Compensation for Improvements 73
How Compensation can be Lost 74
Ulster Tenant Right 74
The Bright Clauses 75
Rack-rents 75, 76
Griffith's Valuation 76
Old Increases of Rent ... ... 77—79
Prices in 1852 and 1875 78
Causes of the Land Act of 1881 79
Mr. Gladstone on the Irish Landlords 80

PAGE

The Land Law (Ireland) Act, 1881 ... ... 80—91
Fixity of Tenure 82
Fair Rent 82
Misrepresentation of Fair Rent 82
What Tenants are excluded 83
Arrears and Fair Rent 84
Judicial Reduction 84, 85
Decline in Prices 86
Reductions vary with Size of Holdings 87, 88
Free Sale ... ... 88—91
Arrears Act, 1882 ... ... 91, 92
Land Purchase Act, 1885 and 1888 ... ... 92—96
Parnellite Misrepresentations of Purchase Act ... 94—96
Land Law Amendment Act, 1887 ... ... 97, 98
The Real Argument from the Land Act... 98
Irish *versus* English Tenants 99
The Parnellites and the Land Acts 100
The Present Position of the Landlord ... ... 101—103
Arrears 104, 105
The Rejection of Mr. Parnell's Bill of 1886 ... ... 105, 106
Evictions 106, 107
The Law of Eviction ... ... 107—109
Facts and Figures of Evictions ... ... 109—113
American Evictions 113
Evictions in the Abstract 114
Are Irish Evictions Unjust? 115
The Glenbeigh Evictions 116
The "Plan of Campaign"... ... ... 117—127
The Massereene Estate 118
The Ponsonby Estate... 119
The Kingston Estate 119
The Luggacurran Estate 120
The O'Grady Estate 121
The Brooke Estate 122
The Vandeleur Estate 123
Summary 126
The Olphert Estate 124
The Kenmare Estate 124
The Smith-Barry Estate 125

PAGE
The Real Object of the Land Movement 128, 129
Mr C. S. Parnell at Galway 128
Mr. T. M. Healy at Boston 128
Mr T. M. Healy at New Orleans 128
Rev. Mr. Cantwell in Dublin... 128
Mr. W. O'Brien in Carrick-on-Suir 128
Mr. T. P. O'Connor in St. Louis, U.S.A 129
Rev. Eugene Sheehy in New York 129
Dr. J. E. Kenny in Dublin 129
Mr. W. O'Brien at Tulla 129
The Irish *Felon* and Michael Davitt 130
The Dublin Corporation 131
The Land-Grabber 132
Savings Banks 133
Summary (Mr. J. Morley) 134

Part III.

COERCION.

Coercion—Three-fold Line of Argument... 134
Coercion a Nickname 135
Mr. T. P. O'Connor on Liberal Coercion 135
Mr. Parnell on Liberal Coercion 135

A. Necessity for a Crimes Act ... ... 136—142
The Evidence of the Judges 136, 137
Mr. Justice O'Brien in Co. Clare 136
Mr. Justice Lawson in Co. Mayo 136
Mr. Justice O'Brien in Co. Kerry 136
Mr. Justice Johnson in Co. Cork 137
Mr. Justice Murphy in Co. Galway 137
Unpunished Crime in 1886 137
Why was Justice Paralysed ?... 138
Witnesses 138
Jurors 139
United Ireland on Jurors 140

PAGE

Coercion the Alternative to Home Rule 141
Mr. J. E. Redmond on Coercion 141
B. The Crimes Act of 1887 ... ... 142—149
Its Provisions ... ... 142—145
Parnellite Fictions about the Crimes Act 145, 146
1. New Offences 145
2. The Law of Conspiracy 145
3. Public Meetings 146
4. Newsvendors 146
5. Incompetent Courts 146
6. The Right of Appeal 146
7. Trades' Union Offences 146
The Crimes Act and Scotch Law ... ... 146—148
1. Preliminary Investigation 147
2. Summary Jurisdiction 147, 148
3. Change of Venue 148
4. Proclamation of Districts 148
Justice of the Crimes Act 148
Mr. Gladstone's Coercion of 1882 ... ... 149—152
Mr. Parnell's Coercion Bill 152
The Results of the Crimes Act 152, 153
Table of Agrarian Crimes 152, 153
Outrages in Clare and Kerry from 1877 to 1888 ... 153

C. The Administration of the Law in Ireland... ... 154—164
Four Parnellite Pleas 154, 155
Irish Prison Rules 155
Parnellite Methods of Dealing with Crimes Act Cases 141—143
Parnellite Fictions about Coercion ... ... 156—164
The Mandeville Fiction 158
The Mitchelstown Fiction 159
The "Cheering" or "Groaning" Fiction ... 160
The Kinsella Fiction 161
The "Laughing" or "Smiling" Fiction 162
The "Brave Little Girl" Fiction 163
The Real Coercion 164
Agrarian Murders 165
Outrages on Kenmare Estate 165
Boycotting, Offences for which it is Inflicted ... 166
What is Boycotting? 167

PAGE
The Initiation of Boycotting 168
Boycotting still the Parnellite Policy 168
Mr. T. W. Rolleston on Boycotting 169, 170
Mr. Gladstone on Boycotting 170
Report of the Cowper Commission on Boycotting ... 170
Cases of Boycotting 171
Statistics of Boycotting 171, 172
Gladstonian Speeches about Coercion ... 172, 173
Respect for the Law a Radical Doctrine 174

Part IV.

SUPPLEMENTAL.

The Parnellites ... ... 175—179
Their Literature ... ... 175—177
Their Speakers... ... ... 178, 179
Mr. John O'Connor, M.P. 178
Mr. John Dillon, M.P. 178
Mr. T. D. Sullivan. M.P. 179
Mr. W. O'Brien, M.P.... 179
Mr. T. P. O'Connor, M.P. 180
List of Useful Books 181
Conclusion 182

THE SPEAKER'S HAND-BOOK

ON

THE IRISH QUESTION.

Part I.

HOME RULE.

DEFINITION OF HOME RULE.

THE phrase HOME RULE will be used invariably in these pages to denote any scheme or policy which involves the establishment of a Parliament in Ireland, together with an Executive Government responsible to that Parliament. It will thus include alike the plan proposed by Mr. Gladstone in 1886—of which a full account is given—and any other scheme under which the control of law and of the judges would be transferred from Imperial to Irish hands. It will alike include any plan under which the Irish Members of Parliament would be either excluded from or retained at Westminster—a subject dealt with in its proper place—or under which the United Kingdom would become a union of federated States.

HOME RULE NOT LOCAL GOVERNMENT.

It will often be the duty of a speaker to impress on his audiences the necessity of clearness of view on this subject. The question of Home Rule has no relation whatever to the question of Local Government. The events of the present year (1889) demonstrate this thoroughly. Every county and every large town in Great Britain is now enabled to control a large proportion of its local affairs. Yorkshire, Lanarkshire, Liverpool, Dundee, and many other places, will henceforth be areas of local administration. All possess Local Government, but none possess Home Rule; for not one of them will have a Cabinet or Prime Minister for itself, nor a set of judges for itself, distinct from the judicial system of the rest of Great Britain.

This distinction is most important, for it at once enables a speaker to put an end to the use of ambiguous phrases. People write and talk of letting Ireland "manage her own affairs," or they speak of "Irish autonomy;" whenever they do, it is a sure sign either that they possess no clear ideas on the subject, or that they wish to confuse the minds of their hearers.

Home Rulers ask for something for Ireland absolutely different from that "management of her own affairs" which now belongs to Lancashire, for example. If any doubt is felt on that point it will be at once dispelled by the citation of the following:—

MR. JOHN DILLON, M.P., ON HOME RULE AND LOCAL GOVERNMENT.

Speaking at Inverness on November 17th, 1887, Mr. John Dillon, M.P., was asked the following questions, to which he gave the subjoined replies:—

Question I.—Keeping in view that both sides in politics in England and Scotland not only desire but insist on decentralisation, and a very large and comprehensive scheme of Local Self-Government, would you not be willing to accept of such a scheme for Ireland also, to see how it worked, with power to improve and develop it by degrees, as circumstances might require?

Answer I.—Certainly not, because I do not think that any scheme short of the Bill of Mr. Gladstone would work good in Ireland, and such a proposal as this would work a great deal of mischief and make the settlement of the question more difficult.

Question II.—Assuming, but not admitting, that the Irish Party do not wish to encroach upon Imperial jurisdiction, do you assert that the Irish people, armed by the Legislature with a full and generous power of local management, cannot obtain the same degree of peace and freedom of action as other civilised communities enjoy?

Answer II.—I certainly do assert it, because one fundamental condition we require is that the administration of the law in Ireland shall be under the control of the representatives of Ireland as well as the making of the laws in Ireland. No system of Local Government will get us that.—(*Inverness Courier*, November 18th, 1887.)

These frank admissions of Mr. Dillon may at once be taken to decide the matter.

Arguments for Home Rule.

The speaker who is called on to address a public meeting is obliged to keep continually before his mind the leading arguments advanced by the supporters of Home Rule. He will meet these arguments not only in the speeches of opponents, but also in questions and interruptions from the audience. It is, therefore, necessary in this Hand-book to enumerate the chief lines of thought and argument adopted by those Home Rulers who are willing to think and argue on this branch of the question, and to state the chief replies to each.

The leading—if not all the—arguments advanced in favour of Home Rule for Ireland may be grouped under the following heads:—

[A] That Home Rule is demanded by a majority of the Irish people.

[B] That England has governed Ireland shamefully in the past, and ought to make amends.

[C] That the Irish people were cheated and robbed of their inherent rights in 1800 by the Act of Union.

[D] That the Legislative Union has been a failure.

[E] That a policy similar to that of Home Rule has been elsewhere successful.

[F] That certain grievances exist in connection with the land question.

[G] That what is called "Coercion" is the only alternative to Home Rule.

Each of these arguments must be met by an answer dealing with actual facts, and they will now be taken in order.

A.—THAT HOME RULE IS DEMANDED BY A MAJORITY OF THE IRISH PEOPLE.

THE Home Rule case in this matter is generally put in the form of a syllogism, which to Home Rulers appears quite irresistible. The argument is this:—

> Majorities should have the form of government they desire.
> The majority of the Irish people desire Home Rule.
> Therefore the majority of the Irish people should have Home Rule.

The truth or falsehood of this conclusion depends entirely upon an assumption underlying the first or major proposition of this argument. It is not true that all majorities should have the form of government they desire.

The matter can best be tested thus. Would the majority of the inhabitants of Yorkshire or of Inverness-shire have the right to govern itself? To that question the answer is obvious. "Yes," as regards Local Government; "No," as regards Home Rule.

It is therefore quite plain that if the answer in the case of Ireland is to be different from that in the case of Yorkshire or of Inverness-shire, it must only be because Ireland stands on a different footing from these counties.

This, of course, is what is asserted by Home Rulers. They say, "There is no analogy between Yorkshire (for example) and Ireland, for Yorkshire is only a part of the larger unit England, while Ireland is itself a unit." In other words, the people of Yorkshire are Englishmen, and must sink or swim with England; but there is a separate Irish people.

It is, of course, possible that a speaker may meet with people who will urge that Yorkshire, for example, would be entitled to a separate Parliament and Executive if the majority of her members should demand it. The present writer has often met with such. They can be easily refuted by pointing out that if a single English county would be entitled to separate treatment on demand of a majority of its electors, the same could not be refused to a single Irish county, and that, therefore, Antrim would be entitled to refuse Home Rule, or to demand it for herself.

It will, however, certainly be found that nineteen Home Rulers out of twenty will maintain that Ireland is entitled to separate treatment, because a majority of what is termed the Irish nation demands it.

To this the Unionist answer is twofold, and is as follows:—

1. *Assuming that there is an "Irish nation," the argument is utterly unsound. Even Home Rulers do not believe that the majority of the Irish nation has a right to choose its own form of government; and*

2. *It is nonsense to talk about the "Irish nation" in face of the historical fact that, just as there are three nations in the island of Great Britain, there are also two nations in Ireland.*

1. It cannot be denied that all Home Rulers base the right of Ireland to ask for Home Rule on the ground that Ireland is a nation. "IRELAND A NATION" is the toast at every Irish Nationalist banquet, whether in Ireland or America.

But what are the rights of a nation?

If Ireland be a nation she is certainly entitled to the rights of a nation. She is entitled to the rights of France, or Germany, or the United States. These rights obviously include the following:—

[A] The right to choose her own form of government, and to say whether it shall be monarchical or republican.

[B] The right to separate from Great Britain altogether, if she chooses, either now or at any time.

[C] The right to her own army and navy and foreign policy.

[D] The right to have colonies of her own, if she can get them.

[E] The right to absolutely control her own trade and taxation; and

[F] The right to establish and endow the Roman Catholic, or any other Church, should she so choose.

These are certainly the rights of nations; but the curious thing is that there is not a single Gladstonian Home Ruler to be found who pretends for an instant that Ireland is entitled to a single one of the national rights we have specified. Not a single one of them believes in the national rights of Ireland.

There are, indeed, some men who do. The extreme American Fenian section do believe in these national rights of Ireland—a fact which shows that, so far as this branch of the subject is concerned, they, and they alone, are the logical Home Rulers.

Home Rulers sometimes try to turn the flank of this argument by urging that Ireland is really a nation, but that no difficulty arises in this matter because she is content to waive those particular national rights which we have specified, and perhaps some others. This contention does not touch the fact that if Ireland be really a nation, she is entitled, either now or at any future time, to claim these rights. No English or Scotch Home Ruler will base his argument for Home Rule on such a position.

It may, however, be urged that what has been said is a dispute about words. Scotland and Wales, it may be said, have no such rights, and yet they are nations—in the sense at all events that they are distinct nationalities from England.

It must be pointed out at once that this consideration does not affect the contention, which is, that national rights are no argument for Home Rule. If Ireland, or Scotland, or Wales, is entitled as a nation or nationality to demand Home Rule, she is, by virtue of the very same authority, entitled any day to claim separation. Nobody, in short, can with reason claim Home Rule for Ireland on the ground of her nationhood, and yet contend that the same nationhood would not give her a claim to separation.

2. Unionists further contend that there is no such thing as "the Irish nation." They say that in any sense in which there is an Irish nation, there are two Irish nations.

It will be conceded by all thinking men that this is of the essence of the entire question. If there be not one, but two Irish nationalities, it is open for people to argue that both ought to remain subject to one Imperial Parliament; or that each nationality should have its own Parliament. It is not open to anybody to say that a Parliament should be given only to one nationality, and that by its instrumentality the other nationality should also be governed. Two important questions must therefore be at once answered, and they are these :—1. What are the marks and signs of a nation? 2. Has Ireland these marks and signs?

THE MARKS AND SIGNS OF A NATION.

It is pretty clear that the things that distinguish one nation from another are after all limited. Probably the following is a complete list:—(1) Geographical Position; (2) Historical Growth; (3) Distinct Origin; (4) Language; (5) Religion; and (6) Possession of Distinct Ideas and Habits. It is practically impossible to think of any other essentials which ought to be taken into account—indeed, some of the subjects specified overlap others. For example, distinct origin or race involves to a large extent diversity of language.

Now the Unionist contention is that, judged by *any* of these indications, the case for a single separate Irish nationality utterly breaks down. There is, however, every reason, judging by the same tokens, to conclude that there exist side by side in Ireland two distinct nationalities. Let us take these different indications in turn.

Has Ireland a Distinct Nationality?

Geographical Position.—It is quite clear that this will not help the Home Rule argument. Great Britain is one island, and Ireland is undoubtedly another. So far, there may be an indication that a distinct nationality is possible. But this is of no use whatever, unless it can be maintained that in one island there is only one nationality, and that quite distinct from the nationality or nationalities in the other. In the island of Great Britain, though *as an island* it is only one, there are three nationalities—the English, the Scotch, and the Welsh. Unless, therefore, it can be proved that there is only one nationality in Ireland, the geographical argument for Home Rule is worthless.

Historical Growth.—Have the facts of history made Ireland a nationality? By no means. Scotland they have made a nation. For centuries Scotland was a separate kingdom. She had her own king and constitution; she made her own laws; she sent her own ambassadors to foreign countries; she had her own army and navy; above all, she had her own independent national life, and her own capital. Some of these things may be true of Wales, but certainly not of Ireland. When the English first entered Ireland, Ireland was not one kingdom, but several; in no real sense (as will be seen in subsequent sections, pp. 19, 20) did Ireland ever make her own laws. Ireland never sent out a foreign embassy, nor had she ever an army or navy, a distinct national existence, or indeed a capital. So much for the purely historical argument.

Distinct Origin. — Many people, however, think that Ireland has a separate existence as a distinct national unit because the Irish are a different race from the English. In the first place, it must at once be pointed out that race proves nothing; for, on the one hand, half a dozen races may often make one nation, and, on the other hand, one race may make half a dozen nations. No one doubts that France is one nation; though there is far more race-difference between an inhabitant of Brittany, an inhabitant of Normandy, and an inhabitant of Provence, than there is between English, Scotch, Irish, and Welsh. On the other hand, Normans, Saxons, and Danes, who have gone to make up the English, have also made up the American nation, which in its turn consists of English, Irish, Germans, Dutch, Swedes, and Negroes. Forgetting all this, however, and assuming that race will make a difference, it must never be forgotten that the larger number of the so-called Irish people are Anglo-Saxon. Thoughtless and inaccurate people speak sometimes of their Celtic origin; but when they do it only displays absolute ignorance. We cite as proof of our statement an authority to whom all Home Rulers should submit, namely, Mr. Gladstone, in words spoken not three years ago, but since he became a Home Ruler himself. Speaking at Liverpool during the crisis of the 1886 election he used these words:—

MR. GLADSTONE ON THE IRISH RACE.

"Are you aware, probably many of you are, that of the population of Ireland by far the greater part is of British descent?" (Speech at Liverpool, *Daily News*, June 26th, 1886.) And by "British" descent Mr. Gladstone clearly meant, if not Anglo-Saxon, at least Anglo-Scotch. For as an illustration of his contention he proceeded to point out that Tipperary—in his opinion, the county which England had found most troublesome—owed its population to English soldiers of the past.

Language.—Language is certainly a great indication of nationality. It is at present possessed by Wales, but not by Ireland. Only a small minority of Irishmen speak Irish. In fact, English is the language of the natives of Ireland, just as it is of the natives of Great Britain.

Religion.—As far as religion comes into the matter at all, it would point to the existence not of one but of two Irish peoples.

Community of Ideas.—It may indeed be urged that in Ireland there is a community of habits and sympathies alien from the English or Scotch communities. That is perfectly true; but as an argument for Home Rule it is at once destroyed by the fact that in Ireland there are two communities, each of alien habits and sympathies from the other.

Minorities must Yield to Majorities.

When the Home Ruler is forced to recognise the existence of a second Irish community, he always tries to escape from his difficulty by saying, "There may be a second Irish community, but it is only a minority, and must yield to the majority." Now, as this is said every day, it is necessary to point out clearly wherein its fallacy lies.

The Whole Question of Majorities Depends on Area.

Whenever we speak of a majority we must mean a majority existing in some area. The Home Ruler says, "The people in the north-east of Ireland must yield, for they are a minority." Strange to say, the Unionist says, "The Irish community must yield, for it is a minority, and the majority of the United Kingdom must rule." The question then is, Of what area do we speak? In Great Britain the English are in a vast majority when compared with the Scotch or Welsh, or with both put together. Are the Scotch and Welsh therefore to give way?

It must at once be conceded even by Scotch Home Rulers that if the 4,000,000 persons who live in Scotland were now dwelling *among* the 25,000,000 who inhabit England, they would have no claim for Home Rule at all, but, being a minority, would have to yield to the English majority. Any claim Scotch or Welsh have to separate treatment must depend on this—that while a small minority of the population of Great Britain, there is, notwithstanding, a part of Great Britain where, instead of being a minority, they are and have been for ages a majority.

This is exactly the consideration which Unionists apply to Ireland. It is perfectly true that over the largest part of Ireland a certain community predominates. It is equally true that over a smaller part a smaller community predominates. The condition of Ireland is exactly analogous to that of Great Britain. As between English and Scotch in the one island it is not a case of majority and minority, but of two distinct communities, each a majority in its own sphere; so in Ireland it is a case not of majority and minority, but of two distinct majorities. The second Irish community—the community, that is, which returns men like Mr. T. W. Russell, M.P., and Colonel Saunderson, M.P., to Parliament—is distinguished from the other community, (1) by a difference in history, (2) by a difference in habits and ideas, (3) by a difference in religion, but (4) lastly, most important, and most frequently forgotten of all, in that it inhabits a different part of Ireland, in which it is numerically supreme. In short, it possesses exactly those same marks of distinction which separate Englishmen from Scotchmen, or Englishmen from Irishmen. If these marks of being a separate people are of any force as arguments for the establishment of a Parliament in Dublin, they are all equally valid for a Parliament in Belfast.

Do the Loyalists Want a Second Parliament?

It is sometimes urged in reply that the Unionist representatives from the North of Ireland want no second Parliament in, say, Belfast. Let there be no misapprehension at all on this point. They want no Parliament in Ireland at all, but they have unmistakably indicated what they as another community do not want, viz., to be governed by a Parliament set up to gratify the community which is not a majority in their part of Ireland. Their wishes may be summed in one phrase :—They will not have their allegiance transferred from Westminster to Dublin.

The Question of Ulster.

A speaker in Great Britain will often find himself confronted by a well-known Home Rule argument. It will be said, "Oh, Ulster joins with the rest of Ireland in asking for Home Rule. There are 17 Nationalist members from Ulster, and only 16 Unionist members."

To this there are two answers. The first is this : that the majority is apparent and not real. The second, which is absolutely conclusive, relates to the past history of the Ulster Plantation.

1. The Nationalist majority in Ulster would never exist at all, only for an anomalous distribution of the seats in Ulster. In that province there are 33 electoral divisions, each returning one member, while the average number of voters is 8,000 per constituency. Two small boroughs, Londonderry and Newry, possessing only 3,800 and 2,100 voters respectively, are, however, allowed to exist and give the Nationalists their majority. The important fact, however, is that at the last General Election (1886) 72,704 electors in Ulster voted for Home Rule, and 88,865 against it. This by itself points to a grossly faulty condition of the representation.

2. There is, however, a still stronger line of argument The second community in Ireland, as we have called the great Unionist body of North-East Ulster, has a separate historical origin. It owes its existence to the Scotch and English colonies, founded for high imperial considerations, in North-East Ulster. The men who form it are the sons and descendants of the original colonists, and within the limits of the original colonies they are in an overwhelming majority.

Donegal, save in the barony of Raphoe, was never a "planted" county, nor were Cavan and Monaghan thoroughly and entirely colonised. When these counties are subtracted, the area of the real Plantation is found. The real strength of the Unionist position lies not in the Ulster of the geographer, but in the Ulster of the historian—that is, in this "Plantation." Within this, its own legitimate sphere, Unionist opinion is easily supreme. The following figures demonstrate it :—

CONSTITUENCIES AND MEMBERS.

	No. of Constituencies.	Home Rulers.	Unionists.
Ulster	33	... 17	16
Plantation	26	10*	16

VOTES GIVEN AT LAST ELECTION.

	For Home Rule.	Unionist.	Unionist Majority.
Ulster ...	72,704	88,865	16.161
Plantation	51,188	... 80,947	29.759

Hence, then, arises the Unionist appeal to the honesty of the electorate. The contention is as follows :—Home Rule need not be granted in deference to any supposed national rights, or in deference to the wishes of the majority of the inhabitants of Ireland. But if we cannot convince you of that, if you still think you must yield to one Irish community, you are also bound to yield to the other, and leave it free, (1) either to join a Dublin Parliament, (2) to continue its representation at Westminster, or (3) to have its own government.

THE CONSTITUTION OF THE IRISH MAJORITY AND MINORITY.

There is another line of argument fairly open to Unionist speakers. It is that which points to the constitution of the Irish majority, and, if it does nothing else, it helps to point to

* Including Londonderry and Newry.

the existence of two communities. The following facts may be borne in mind:—

1. At the General Election of 1886 exactly half the Irish electorate voted for Home Rule, but no more. The other half voted against it or abstained.

2. The names of all the principal commercial men in Ireland are conspicuous by their absence from every list of Home Rulers that has ever seen the light. Mr. Parnell is followed neither by bankers, brewers, millers, timber merchants, linen merchants, cloth merchants, stockbrokers, shipbuilders, engineers, monster shopkeepers, booksellers, or hotel-keepers. A few solitary names alone can be found from such quarters.

3. The only working-men in Ireland who correspond at all in their habits and methods of life and employment to those in English and Scotch industrial centres are overwhelmingly against Home Rule. The city of Belfast has its electorate almost entirely composed of such working-men, and its vote at the last election was as follows—for Home Rule, 6,460; against, 17,861. Majority against, 11,401.

4. The vast majority of the educated classes are against Home Rule, while Mr. Parnell is supported by thousands of voters who can neither read nor write. To such an extent is this the case that out of every 6 electors in Ireland, one is unable to mark his cross on a balloting paper. At the last General Election out of 194,994 voters 36,722 were illiterate. In England and Wales, on the contrary, out of 2,416,272 voters, there were only 38,587 illiterates, or only one voter in 62. Wherever there are many illiterates there is a Parnellite member returned by an overwhelming majority. Thus the one-fourth

of the County Donegal which returns Mr. Swift MacNeill, M.P., has as many of these poor ignorant voters as the whole kingdom of Scotland. The three Unionist members for Belfast, representing 23,000 voters, have 1,500 illiterates in their divisions; but Mr. Sexton, M.P., the fourth member, a Nationalist, represents 8,600 voters, of whom 1,852 are illiterate.

5. There are 1,173,600 Protestants in Ireland; but there are not 5,000 Protestant Home Rulers, including women, infants, and lunatics.

6. The Church of Ireland (Protestant Episcopal) numbers 639,500 members, and its General Synod has unanimously declared against Home Rule.

7. The Presbyterian Church in Ireland, numbering 470,700, has with equal unanimity declared against Home Rule.

8. The governing bodies of the Methodist, Baptist, and Non-subscribing Presbyterians have also with practical unanimity protested against Home Rule.*

9. The members of the Chambers of Commerce in both Belfast and Dublin have also protested; as have the members of the Board and Senate of the University of Dublin.

These considerations will, at least, appeal to the minds of those who hold that majorities should be weighed as well as counted.

* The presentation in November, 1888, of an address to Lords Salisbury and Hartington showed that out of 990 non-Episcopal ministers in Ireland only 8 were Home Rulers. It may also be pointed out that the Protestant community in Ireland is sometimes assumed to be "Orange," but it includes 100,000 adult Liberals, while the members of the Orange Society number less than 50,000. On the other hand, the Protestant Home Rulers are so few that they are unable to hold public meetings without the assistance of a Roman Catholic audience.

B.—ENGLAND HAS GOVERNED IRELAND SHAMEFULLY IN THE PAST, AND OUGHT TO MAKE AMENDS BY GRANTING HOME RULE.

This argument, in one form or another, is continually making its appearance. For it there is one answer, and that will be found in an accurate knowledge of the leading facts of Irish history. These leading facts will now be placed in convenient form for the benefit of inquirers. It will probably be advisable to preface them with an accurate list of the leading dates :—

Important Dates in Connection with the History of Ireland.

A.D.

1170. Invasion of the Anglo-Norman barons.
1367. Statute of Kilkenny.
1376. Anglo-Irish clergy and laity summoned to Westminster.
1390. English Pale limited to four counties.
1494. Poynings' Law.
1580. Ireland invaded by Spain.
1593. Tyrone demands the expulsion of the settlers.
1598. The English obliged to fly.
1601–3. Lord Mountjoy conquers Ireland.
1611–15. Plantation of Ulster.
1632. Strafford becomes Viceroy.
1641. The Great Rebellion.
1650. Cromwell subdues Ireland.
1661. Charles II. passes an Act of Settlement.
1687. Tyrconnel Viceroy. Ruin of the Protestants.
1689–96. Arrival of William III. Penal Laws.
1707. Ireland begs for a Union like that passed this year with Scotland.
1782. Grattan's Parliament.
1793. Admission of Roman Catholics to the Franchise.

1798. Rebellion.
1800. Act of Union passed.*

Important Points in Irish History.

It is by no means intended in the succeeding pages to write anything approaching a history of Ireland; all that will be attempted is to give information which will correct popular errors and every-day fallacies about that history.

The Kingdom of Ireland.

In 1170, in the reign of Henry II., certain English barons undertook to conquer Ireland. They found there five kingdoms, but no one Celtic State called Ireland, Hibernia, Erin, or anything else. Ireland was not a kingdom till England made her one. *It is often said that England has oppressed Ireland for 700 years*, but from 1170 until at least 1600 England did not own or interfere with three-fourths of Ireland. From 1170 for many centuries Ireland was practically divided into two parts—one inhabited by English colonists, and the other, which was much larger, by tribes who had no central or settled government. Henry VIII. constituted Ireland a kingdom.

Ireland and Civilisation.

Ireland had been the seat of an ancient civilisation. Many men of considerable learning, culture, and piety inhabited her monasteries in very early times. Long before a single Englishman ever planted foot in Ireland, that civilisation died utterly. It is as well to recollect that everything of law, politics, and freedom Ireland possesses has come to her from without—from England.

The Early Population of Ireland.

As has been already pointed out, there is reason to believe the majority of the people of Ireland to be of Anglo-Saxon descent.

* For later dates, from Act of Union up to present time, *see* p. 27.

This, however, is of course only true now; it could not be true of the days before the English entered Ireland. Sir John Davies, however, who was Attorney-General of Ireland in the time of James I., emphatically tells us it was so then; and Mr. Gladstone, at Liverpool, in June, 1886, quoted his words with approval. But it is a *fatal and popular blunder to imagine that even before the arrival of the English there was a Celtic State in Ireland.* The Danes had settled already on the east, and the Spaniards on the west. So little was Ireland the country of the Celtic Irish that hardly a single town of importance in Ireland had a Celtic origin. The Danes built Dublin, Drogheda, Wexford, and Waterford; the Normans built Cork and Limerick; the Spaniards built Galway; while Derry and Belfast are the creation of English and Scotch settlers.

The English Pale.

The part of Ireland inhabited by the first settlers was called the English Pale. In the days of John this "Pale" was far less than half the country. In Ulster, Connaught, and the non-maritime parts of Munster and Leinster the Irish were left unmolested. In the reign of Richard II. this "Pale" consisted of only four counties—Dublin, Meath, Kildare, and Louth—or less than one-tenth of Ireland, the other nine-tenths being in the hands of the non-English population.

Home Rule Nonsense about Invaders.

A great deal of nonsense is often talked about the English settlers in Ireland being invaders and interlopers. Of course they were, but that does not afford any reason whatever for clearing their descendants out of the country. The Celtic Irish themselves were once interlopers, who so treated their predecessors in occupation that hardly any trace of them is to be found. Besides, if this is to be the rule, why confine it to Ireland? On such a theory the English should not only retire from Ireland, but from England, which they once took from the ancient Britons, whose descendants are still living in Wales. The entire white people, both English and Irish, who live in the United States ought, on that principle, to send all American negroes back to Africa and come to Europe themselves, so as to leave America to the Red Indians, to whom it once undoubtedly belonged.

THE OLD IRISH PARLIAMENT.

The old Irish Parliament was, in its origin, simply a Parliament of the English settlers in Ireland. It had no connection whatever in early days with the non-English population. The Statute of Kilkenny will illustrate this conclusively; it was passed by the so-called "Irish" Parliament in 1367, and under it English subjects in Ireland were forbidden to intermarry with the native Irish under the penalties of High Treason. It is interesting to recollect that in 1376 Edward III. summoned the Irish clergy and laity (*i.e.*, the English clergy and laity in Ireland, whom we shall henceforth call the ANGLO-IRISH) to send deputies to the Parliament at Westminster, which they did.

POYNINGS' LAW.

To understand Poynings' Law, which is almost always spoken of now as a piece of English oppression, it must be remembered that early in the reign of Henry VII. the impostor Lambert Simnel appeared. He was crowned king in Christ Church Cathedral, Dublin, and he forthwith convened a Parliament which wreaked vengeance on all his opponents. It was a Parliament of certain Anglo-Irish and others who followed him, and it proceeded to punish those who remained loyal to Henry. When Simnel was crushed, the Act called Poynings' Law, from the Deputy (or Lord-Lieutenant) of the day, was passed. It provided "that Parliaments should not be holden in Ireland until the King's lieutenant and council had notified to the

King, under the Great Seal of that land, the causes and considerations, and all such Acts as to them seemeth should pass in the same Parliament; nor until such causes, and acts, and considerations had been affirmed by the King or his council to be good and expedient, or license to summon Parliament had been given under the Great Seal of England." It was passed, not to enslave the native Irish, *with whom it had nothing to do*, but at the request of the Anglo-Irish, to protect them from such a Lord-Deputy as had been the Earl of Kildare, who had connived at Simnel's coronation. The little English colony begged for the Act, in order that no laws might in future be passed by a Viceroy without the knowledge of the Sovereign. Hence the consent of the English Privy Council was for long regarded as necessary to measures passed by the Anglo-Irish.

Ireland under Elizabeth.

Ireland would, perhaps, never have been reduced by English troops but for the Pope and Philip II. of Spain. In 1579 they despatched a force to Ireland to strike at Elizabeth. The Earl of Desmond joined them, carrying with him the native Irish. They were, however, utterly routed by Lord Grey de Wilton, Desmond's estates were forfeited, and a Parliament sitting in Dublin allotted them to English settlers. These settlers were called "undertakers," because they undertook to reside on the lands. In 1593 fresh troubles arose, this time in the north, when Hugh O'Neil, Earl of Tyrone, demanded the expulsion of all English settlers and officials, and looked for aid to Spain. He roused the native Irish, with whom many of the earlier settlers joined, the rebellion became widespread, and Elizabeth's "undertakers" had to fly. In 1601 the Spaniards arrived, but Lord Mountjoy completely defeated them, and reduced the whole country. The year 1603, the same that witnessed the union of the crowns of England and Scotland, saw the first conquest of all Ireland.

THE REFORMATION IN IRELAND.

It is possible--and, indeed, likely—that but for religion there would not now be an Irish Question. Conquerors and conquered have existed at all times and in all countries, and, save where some powerful disintegrating element was at work, such as a religious difference, they have usually coalesced. The Reformation, however, brought a new quarrel into Ireland. The earlier English settlers remained Roman Catholic, and amalgamated easily with the native Irish, becoming, in the language of the old proverb, "More Irish than the Irish themselves;" but the later settlers, being Protestants, never so amalgamated. The old quarrel was superseded by another.

THE PLANTATION OF ULSTER.

This was the most memorable feature of the reign of James I. On the death of Elizabeth much opposition was shown to James, and especially in Ulster. Accordingly, to check rebellion, the lands of certain northern counties were taken by the Crown, and three-quarters of a million of acres were granted on favourable terms to settlers. The citizens of London received large grants in the county of Derry, and made Derry city—henceforth Londonderry—the leading town of the extreme north. Protestant colonists from Scotland and England were encouraged to settle in 1611, and again on a large scale in 1615.

STRAFFORD IN IRELAND.

With the odious English politics of the Earl of Strafford we have nothing to do, but he undoubtedly benefited Ireland. He increased the revenues, improved trade, and administered justice; most important of all, he mainly founded the Ulster linen trade, bringing over flax-seed from Holland and encouraging Flemish workmen. His action towards the woollen trade was not equally beneficent. Like all other Englishmen of the period, he thought he saw in it a rival to English trade. It is, however, well to recollect that this woollen trade was absolutely created by the Irish Protestant settlers. They, and not the native Irish, were ruined by its suppression. All such incidents arose from the fact that there were *two* Governments and *two* opposing interests.

The Great Rebellion.

When the strong hand of Strafford was removed, rebellion appeared. To a large extent it was a war of religion, for religion had consolidated the native Irish. On all sides they rose against the settlers, whose extermination seemed certain, as Charles I., then in difficulties with his Parliament, could give them no succour. Men, women, and children perished in terrible massacres, which were not paralleled in English history until the Indian Mutiny.

Oliver Cromwell.

Cromwell crushed this rebellion. The Irish had inflicted fearful cruelties on the settlers, and Cromwell now punished them with fearful cruelty. Yet in one respect it was a merciful policy, for his unsparing severity at Drogheda and Wexford at once caused all opposition to subside. But Cromwell's legislative arrangements were even more important than his campaign. He at once saw that a Legislative Union was a necessity to the peace of Ireland, so he provided that the Anglo-Irish should send thirty representatives to Westminster. In Cromwell's view the entire Irish difficulty was religious, so he resolved to drive the Roman Catholics back to Connaught and to Clare. The broad stream of the Shannon was to be the border. Thousands of them went abroad, and we subsequently find their names in the record of foreign military service. Cromwell planted their confiscated lands with settlers drawn from every class and creed in Great Britain. Tipperary, for example, was peopled by his soldiers; and the Joyce country in Galway takes its name from the family of one of Cromwell's troopers. When Cromwell died, more than half the population of Ireland must have been Anglo-Saxon by descent. It was, indeed, so in the reign of James I., according to Sir John Davies, before a single Cromwellian could have settled in the country.

Ireland under Charles II.

Charles II. modified the Cromwellian policy by an Act of Settlement passed in 1661 by a Dublin Parliament. This body restored their lands to all former owners who had not taken part in the rebellion and massacres of 1641; yet more than two-thirds of the land remained in the hands of the Protestant minority, who were probably not more than one-fifth of the population. Worse still was the fact that the Roman Catholics were exiled from all share in the government of their native land. It is, indeed, absolutely true that the majority of the Irish people, whether of Celtic or Anglo-Saxon race, had to submit to a tyranny from the minority, on whom the sole restraining influence was the Imperial Government.

Ireland under James II.

James II. proceeded to reverse all this. His object, unfortunately, was not to preserve an equal balance between the two communities, but to make the Roman Catholics supreme in Ireland as in England. In 1687 he made the Earl of Tyrconnel Viceroy, and the work began. The Protestant militia was deprived of muskets. All judges and sheriffs were selected from the Roman Catholics. Fear seized the settlers, who were threatened at once with loss of life, liberty, and land. At first they retreated before a great popular Roman Catholic outbreak, but at the walls of Derry they rallied and triumphed in the greatest siege of history. "The aim of the popular movement was," writes Mr. J. R. Green, "the ruin of the English settlers. The Act of Settlement, on which all property rested, was at once repealed.

Three thousand Protestants of name and fortune were massed together in the highest Bill of Attainder the world has ever seen." Seventy-three peers and nearly all the Commons were condemned to death without any trial, simply because they were Protestants. Eighty-five knights and baronets, 83 clergymen, 22 ladies, and 2,182 esquires were condemned to be butchered by the Roman Catholic Parliament of James II.

The Penal Laws.

It was little wonder, then, that the Protestant Parliament of William III. took good care to protect itself. It adopted two measures :—First, the Penal Laws; and secondly, it petitioned for a Union. Under the Penal Laws the Roman Catholics of Ireland were rigorously excluded not only from all share in the government of their native land, but from its most important liberties. Writing of the two hostile camps in Ireland, Edmund Burke at a later day said : "One of these bodies was to possess *all* the franchises, *all* the property, *all* the education; the other was to be composed of hewers of wood and cutters of turf for them." This code was absolutely in itself indefensible, but four things must always be remembered about it :—

1. It was passed, not by a Westminster, but by a Dublin Parliament.
2. In the Parliaments that passed the Penal Laws there was scarcely a single member whose sufferings at the hands of the other side were not incomparably greater than those he now proposed to inflict.
3. The Irish Penal Laws had their counterpart in England itself, and were chiefly copied from the laws in force against Protestants in Roman Catholic countries.
4. As soon as the terror caused by the Bill of Attainder had died away, the Penal Laws died also, and though remaining in the Statute Book were not, save to a very small extent, put in force.

Roman Catholic Disabilities.

Neither must it be forgotten that the position of Irish Roman Catholics has been grossly misrepresented and their disabilities exaggerated. The favourite Separatist trick on this, as on all historical points, is to judge every Irish episode *as if its parallel was not to be found outside Ireland itself.* Thus a recent Home Rule pamphlet begins with the wrongs Ireland suffered from King John, as if England did not suffer the same, or worse. As a matter of fact, an Irish Roman Catholic was in a far better position from 1793 to 1832 than his English or Scotch co-religionist. In the latter countries he was excluded from the franchise and from office. In Ireland he had the franchise, and was admissible to most civil and military places of trust. For Irish, though not for English or Scotch, Roman Catholics the Test and Corporation Acts had been repealed. In England less than eighty years ago a Roman Catholic could not take a university degree, or become a member of a corporation, or rise in the Army or Navy above the rank of a lieutenant. In Ireland there were no such prohibitions. *In no country in the world where there was an established religion did the Nonconformist enjoy the privileges of the Irish Roman Catholic.* Even an English Presbyterian, though a member of a Church established by law in Scotland, had, in order to qualify for any English office, to take the sacrament according to the rites of the Church of England! But nowadays everything contrary to modern ideas and enlightenment which was done in Ireland in the past is proclaimed to be an Irish grievance: as if all other countries enjoyed free and upright government, or as if the history of every state in the world was not stained, even within the past century, with episodes of wrong.

Ireland from 1700 to 1782.

The history of Ireland during the earlier part of the eighteenth century tells us of a desire for a Legislative Union.

In 1707 the Dublin Parliament prayed for it, but Queen Anne and her Ministers foolishly closed their ears. They had just in that year assented to a union with Scotland, because they thought a Parliament in that country *co-ordinate* with the English Parliament was dangerous; while they thought, as other people have since done, that a *subordinate* Parliament in Dublin could do no harm. Both parties in Ireland wanted a union urgently—the Protestants for security, the Roman Catholics to get rid of the Penal Laws.

Grattan's Parliament.

By 1782 a different state of feeling had grown up among the Protestants. In 1775 the North American States had secured their independence, and this was not without effect on Ireland. Poynings' Law had become a source of offence, as had a statute known as the 6th of George I., by which the English Parliament claimed the right to legislate for Ireland. The Parliament of Anglo-Irish in Dublin, led by Grattan and Flood, demanded independence. Ireland, it was for the first time insisted, had a right to a separate national existence, united to England only by the link of the Crown. The English Ministry yielded, and for the first time in history an absolutely independent Anglo-Irish Parliament sat. It was, of course, exclusively a Protestant Parliament; but one of its earliest measures was to give Roman Catholics the right to buy freehold land, to teach in schools, and to educate their children. The following facts about Grattan's Parliament (as it is often now called) must be carefully remembered:—

1. It was a legislative assembly without a corresponding Executive. The Irish Parliament could not turn the Irish Government out of office.
2. It could, however, at any time, have paralysed Great Britain by refusing to join in any war in which the latter was engaged, or by refusing supplies; and

3. It could have (as was actually proposed) put prohibitive duties on British commerce, and provoked a war of tariffs.
4. It quarrelled directly with the British Parliament on the question of the Regency Bill; and a disastrous split was only prevented by the convalescence of George III. In this matter it acted in absolute contravention of the laws regulating the connection between the two countries, which were only "paper guarantees."
5. It admitted Roman Catholics to the franchise, but refused, by 170 to 30, to admit them to Parliament or public offices.
6. It passed in 18 years no less than 54 Coercion Acts, or three *per annum*.
7. Under this Parliament Ireland was, as we shall see later on, reduced to beggary.
8. Matters culminated in the rebellion of 1798, which had its share in intensifying in Ireland the feelings between Protestant and Catholic. It quickly, as of old, became a religious war, and had its share in inducing Pitt to introduce his measure for a Legislative Union.

Imperial Government since the Union.

How the United Parliament has governed Ireland since 1800 will be apparent to all who read of the Land Legislation passed in the last 20 years (*see* Part II.). The following list of measures passed since the Act of Union should prove useful:—

1829. Roman Catholic Emancipation.
1831. National System of Education, under which every child can be educated at the expense of the State.
1835. Roman Catholic priests allowed to celebrate marriage.
1838. Tenants relieved of tithes by Tithes Commutation Act.
1840. Municipal Reform Act.

1842. Poor Relief Act.
1845. Queen's Colleges (open to all sects) established.
1847. £10,000,000 spent. Relief works for potato famine.
1849. Incumbered Estates Act—facilities for purchase.
1858. Abolition of property qualification for M.P.'s.
1867. Religious Disabilities Act. Lord Chancellor may be a Roman Catholic.
1868. Reform Act.
1869. Disestablishment of Irish Church.
1870. Landlord and Tenant Act. (Compensation for Improvements, etc.)
1878. Intermediate Education Act—for endowing schools
1879. Royal University established.
1881. Land Law Act (Fair Rent, Free Sale, Fixity of Tenure).
1882. Arrears Act.
1883. Light Railways Act.
1885. Land Purchase Act. (Ashbourne Act.)
1885. Reform Act. (Extended franchise to householders.)
1887. Land Act.
1888. Renewal of Ashbourne Act.
1889. Light Railways Act.

It may be mentioned in addition that £38,000,000 of public money has been advanced to Ireland for public works, and of which £7,000,000 has been absolutely forgiven.

C.—THE IRISH PEOPLE WERE CHEATED OF THEIR NATIONAL RIGHTS THROUGH THE PASSING OF THE ACT OF UNION IN 1800.

THIS argument is one which weighs powerfully with a certain class of individuals. It is as well to state at once that the entire contention depends upon two gross and palpable fictions, which have no historical basis whatever. These fictions are—

1. That the Act of Union was carried in violation of the wishes of the Irish people; and

2. That the Act of Union was carried by means of bribery and corruption.

These absurd fallacies must be dealt with separately.

First Fiction.—"Against the Consent of the Irish People."

No more impudent perversion of the truth than this can be imagined. In 1800 the enormous majority of the inhabitants of Ireland were in favour of the Act of Union. The entire opposition to the measure came from some of the Protestants, who in all only numbered 800,000 out of 5,000,000. This can be easily understood; Grattan's Parliament was a Protestant institution by origin and history. On the other hand, almost

The Entire Roman Catholic Population was in Favour of the Act of Union.

Proof. Nothing will illustrate this plain historical fact better than the conduct of the Roman Catholic prelates. All the Archbishops—Dublin, Armagh, Cashel, and Tuam—were, *with their clergy*, in favour of the Union. The entire body of the bishops *unanimously* took the same side, taking with them *their* clergy and the enormously preponderating voice of the laity. Plowden, a Roman Catholic writer, tells us distinctly that this was so, and a glance at the contemporary press will set at rest the doubts of the most suspicious. Practically unanimous petitions went up from the towns of the Catholic West and South. The Roman Catholics of Waterford, of Cork, of Wexford, of Tipperary, of Cahir, of Kilkenny, of Monasterevan, of Longford, of Dundalk, of New Ross, of Limerick, of Roscommon, of Leitrim, and of other places too numerous to name, petitioned for the Union.

This fact would perhaps not be doubted but for an absurd statement made by the younger Grattan, and perpetually quoted by Home Rulers—among others, by Mr. Swift McNeill, M.P. The younger Grattan wrote as follows:—"Only 7,000 persons petitioned in favour of the Union, and 110,000 freeholders and 707,000 persons signed petitions against the measure." It is a piece of good fortune that these numbers bear their own absurdity on their face. We shall take two of his numbers. First, there were 74 petitions at least, in favour of the Union, and *four of them alone*—those from Wexford City and the counties of Leitrim, Tyrone, and Roscommon—were signed by 9,330 persons. So the younger Grattan's statement as to those for the Union is simply false. Now for his 707,000 persons who signed against it. In all Ireland in 1800, had the country been unanimous, there were not enough persons. The total population was only 5,000,000. Of these, about half would be children and young persons; that leaves 2,500,000 adults. Of these, half would be women, and there never has been any pretence that they signed; that leaves 1,250,000. Of these, 250,000 would be Protestants, the remaining 1,000,000 Roman Catholics. Now in 1800 not nearly 50 per cent. of the Protestants could write, nor nearly 15 per cent. of the Roman Catholics. That would give us, in case all Ireland were unanimous, not more than 275,000 possible signatures against the Union; while we know for a fact that the Roman Catholic laity were, with their clergy, for it.* Of similar materials are dozens of Home Rule versions of history constructed.

There is, however, an additional fact which settles all controversy beyond yea or nay. The Irish constituencies were either borough or county. The boroughs were indeed *close*, being generally owned by some patron who sent his nominee to Parliament; but the counties were absolutely *free*. Before

* It may be urged that illiterates signed by making their marks. This can hardly be maintained in view of the fact that the bishops and clergy signed on behalf of their flocks *for the Act of Union*; or in face of the well-known fact that illiterate Irish voters almost invariably vote with their priests. In any case the *facts* about the petitions from the West and South are ample.

1793 only Protestants had the power of voting. In that year the Roman Catholics got the franchise, and this in such a liberal measure that in the counties of the South and West they largely outnumbered the Protestants. For example, when the franchise was Protestant, Cork county had 3,000 voters; when it was open to Roman Catholics there were 20,000. Before 1793, Galway county had 700 voters; after it, 4,000. It was the Roman Catholics of Ireland who elected the members who sat in the Irish Parliament for Clare, Cork, Kerry, Limerick, Tipperary, and Waterford (that is, for all the counties of Munster); also for Mayo, Galway, Longford, Westmeath, Wexford, and other counties. In 1800 the members for the counties we have named (and we have omitted others where the Protestants might possibly have polled a majority of voters) *voted for the Act of Union.* In 1801 they went to their Roman Catholic constituents to get elected to the United Parliament, and by these Roman Catholic constituents they were ALL re-elected.

Second Fiction.—Bribery and Corruption.

Of a similar kind is the talk one hears about bribery and corruption. This accusation is not made, like the last, by inventing falsehoods, but by suppressing facts. It is quite true that £1,260,000 was spent to pass the Act of Union. It is quite true that in those days there existed both in Ireland and England boroughs which were regarded as being the property of their patrons. By the Act of Union this property was abolished, and the owners—as they then were—obtained compensation for the loss of their vested interests. Such a thing is happily impossible at present, for now we have no pocket boroughs. It is, however, easy to demonstrate that what happened in 1800 was free from the smallest taint of bribery. Bribery is to give a man money for voting in a particular way. These men, however, got their money—NO MATTER HOW THEY VOTED. The Parnellite, who is always denouncing these money payments as bribery, has never yet had the honesty to give the people the benefit of the following list:—

List of Moneys Paid to People who Voted *Against* the Act of Union.

The Duke of Leinster . .	£28,000	Lord Belvedere	£7,500
The Marquis of Downshire	52,000	Right Hon. Mr. Ponsonby	15,000
Lord Granard	30,000	Sir John Parnell	7,500
Lord Belmore	30,000	Mr. Tighe.	30,000
Lord Lismore	22,500	Sir John Freke	15,000
Lord Charlemont . . .	15,000	Mr. La Touche	15,000
Lord Kingston	15,000	Mr. Gustavus Lambert .	15,000
Lord Arran	15,000	The Buxton family . . .	15,000
Lord Ludlow	7,500	The King family . . .	15,000
		Mr. Henry Coddington .	7,000

The Speaker—a strong opponent—also received £7,500.

In all, £434,000 was voted by Government to men who were bitter opponents of the Act of Union; while £176,000 went to persons utterly unconnected with politics. Was this bribery? Nor do the Parnellites ever tell their dupes how Grattan and the Opposition raised a fund of £100,000 for undisguised bribery on the other side.

Creation of Peerages.

It is, however, further urged that the Union was obtained by other corrupt means, and notably by a wholesale creation of titles. It should be explained that William Pitt did reward some of his supporters, though, circumstances considered, not so lavishly as even Mr. Gladstone has rewarded his. Most of Pitt's followers, by passing the Act, *put an end to their own political existence.* Out of 300 members of the Irish House of Commons, only 100 could go to the Imperial Parliament; out of a large House of Irish Peers, only twenty-eight could go to Westminster. There was hardly an opponent of the Union of any consequence who was not promoted or advanced after 1800, as were Plunket, Ponsonby, Foster, Saufin, Bushe, Curran, and scores of others. Had these men been in favour of the Union, this would have been called corruption.

Enough has surely been said to enable any one to reply to the preposterous historical arguments of the Home Rule party. [For further information, *see* "History of the Irish Legislative Union," by T. Dunbar Ingram, LL.D., published by Macmillan & Co.]

D.—THAT THE LEGISLATIVE UNION HAS BEEN A FAILURE.

To this it may be answered, in the first place, that it is impossible to call the Act of Union a failure unless we compare it with what went before. This drives us to an examination of the state of Ireland when Government felt obliged to bring in the Act of Union.

LORD CLARE ON THE STATE OF IRELAND IN 1800.

The following extracts from the speech of Lord Clare, Lord High Chancellor of Ireland, delivered on the 10th of February, 1800, ought to be sufficient evidence of the state of Ireland at the time of the passing of the Act of Union :—

"I will now appeal to every dispassionate man who hears me whether I have in anything misstated or exaggerated the calamitous situation of my country, or the coalition of vice and folly which has long undermined her happiness, and at this hour loudly threatens her existence. It is gravely inculcated, I know : 'Let the British Minister leave us to ourselves, and we are very well as we are.' 'We are very well as we are.' Gracious God! of what materials must the heart of that man be composed, who knows the state of the country, and will coldly tell us 'we are very well as we are'? 'We are very well as we are.' *We have not three years of redemption from bankruptcy or intolerable taxation, nor one hour's security against the renewal of exterminating civil war.* 'We are very well as we are.' Look to your statute book—session after session have you been compelled to enact laws of unexampled rigour and novelty to repress the horrible excesses of the mass of your people; and the fury of murder and pillage and desolation have so outrun all legislative exertion that you have been at length driven to the hard necessity of breaking down the pale of the municipal law, and putting your country under the ban of military government; and in every little circle of dignity and independence we hear whispers of discontent at the temperate discretion with which it is administered. 'We are very well as we are.' Look at the old revolutionary Government of the Irish Union, and the modern revolutionary Government of the Irish consulate, canvassing the dregs of that rebel democracy for a renewal of popular ferment and outrage to overcome the deliberations of Parliament. 'We are very well as we are.' Look to your civil and religious dissensions—look to the fury of political faction, and the torrents of human blood that stain the face of your country, and of what material is that man composed who will not listen with patience and goodwill to any proposition that can be made to him for composing the distractions, and healing the wounds, and alienating the miseries of this devoted nation? 'We are very well as we are.' *Look to your finances, and, I repeat, you have not redemption for three years from public bankruptcy, or a burthen of taxation which will sink every gentleman of property in the country.*

* * * * *

"We raise a revenue of more than £230,000 on British goods imported into Ireland; and in return the revenue raised by England on the importation of Irish produce is little more than £10,000. And what are the offerings of gratitude and duty on our part in return for these benefits and advantages? A declaration of war by any foreign Power against the British nation is the signal for faction and rebellion in Ireland. The received maxim is, not to forego the opportunity of foreign war to press forward Irish claims, and ripen every difference and discontent with the British Government into a ground of permanent and rancorous national hostility; insomuch that, in time of difficulty and danger Great Britain, so far from deriving support or security from her connection with Ireland, feels it as a millstone hung upon her neck. * * * *

"Another argument against a Legislative Union is, that it will drive your nobility and gentry from their own country; and practically impoverish the metropolis. With respect to emigration, look to the number of Irish emigrants who now crowd every village in Great Britain, and have been driven to seek an asylum there from the brutal fury of the Irish people, and the cold-blooded treachery of their own domestics, palpably fomented and encouraged by Irish faction and Irish treason. And let any dispassionate man say whether the evil of emigration can ever be greater than it is at this day. If we are to live in a perpetual storm here; if it is to remain at the discretion of every adventurer, of feeble and ostentatious talents, ungoverned by a particle of judgment or discretion, to dress up fictitious grievances for popular delusion, and let loose a savage and barbarous people upon the property and respect of the Irish nation—what gentleman who has the means of living out of this country will be induced to remain in it?"

It is impossible for any man to read this and contend for an instant that the condition of Ireland before the Act of Union was passed was one calculated to give satisfaction to lovers of their country.

Home Rulers, however, tell us that the Act of Union has been a failure. When we ask them how they make that out, they tell us that its failure is detected in the following circumstances:—

1. The decline of the population of Ireland.
2. The failure of Ireland to share in the commercial prosperity of Great Britain.
3. The failure of the Union to secure the consent of those who are governed under it.
4. The fact that, since the Act of Union, about 87 "Coercion" Acts have been passed.

It is necessary for a speaker to obtain accurate information on each of these points, for on each of them a complete answer is forthcoming.

1. The Decline of the Population of Ireland.

The following figures give the census returns for each of the three kingdoms since 1801:—

	England and Wales.	Scotland.	Ireland.
1801	... 8,392,536	... 1,608,420	... No Government census till 1821, but population at time of Act of Union universally estimated as about 5,000,000.
1811	... 10,164,256	... 1,805,864	...
1821	... 12,000,236	... 2,091,521	... 6,801,827
1831	... 13,896,797	... 2,364,286	... 7,767,401

	England and Wales.	Scotland.	Ireland.
1841	... 15,914,148	... 2,620,184	... 8,175,124
1851	... 17,927,609	... 2,888,742	... 6,574,278
1861	... 20,066,224	... 3,062,294	5,798,967
1871	... 22,712,266	3,360,018	... 5,412,377
1881	... 25,974,439	... 3,735,873	... 5,174,836

Now these figures show two things distinctly :—First, that the population of Ireland is decreasing, while that of Great Britain is increasing ; secondly, that the Act of Union has got nothing whatever to say to this, *inasmuch as from* 1821 *till* 1841, *at all events, the population of Ireland increased just as rapidly as that of the rest of the United Kingdom.*

But every thinking man knows the causes of the decline of the population of Ireland. England and Scotland have increased in population simply because of the growth of the great manufacturing centres, which in turn owe their commerce to the coal and iron fields of Great Britain. Ireland has neither coal nor iron worth the working, and no commercial centres, save in one part of the country, which always goes to prove the Unionist contention, as we shall presently see. It may be interesting to know, in corroboration of this, that in every purely agricultural part of Great Britain there is also a decrease in population.

COUNTIES WHICH ARE DECREASING IN POPULATION.

England and Wales.	Scotland.
Cambridge.	Berwick.
Cornwall.	Caithness.
Dorset.	Kincardine.
Hereford.	Kinross.
Hunts.	Orkney.
Rutland.	Ross.
Salop.	Sutherland.
Westmoreland.	Wigton.
Brecon.	
Cardigan.	
Montgomery.	
Pembroke.	
Radnor.	

Those towns in Ireland which are centres of industry as distinguished from merely agricultural markets are increasing in size, as is the total town population of places with a population of over 10,000. In 1841, 17 towns had a population of more than 10,000, and an aggregate of 621,003 inhabitants. In 1881, 19 towns had this population, and an aggregate of 814,926.

The following facts, however, demonstrate with still greater force that the Act of Union has nothing whatever to say to the decline in the population of Ireland :—

Belfast Under the Act of Union.

In 1800 the population of Belfast was 25,000.
In 1850 „ „ „ 70,000.
In 1887 „ „ „ 220,000.

Is this also a consequence of the Act of Union? Belfast has thriven under exactly the same Union and laws as those under which Cork or Limerick decline. At the time of the Act of Union these latter cities were far ahead of it, and it has had no privilege whatever since. We must look elsewhere—to the character of the people—for the cause.

2. Commercial Progress in Ireland.

Much that has been said under the previous head is also relevant here. But what are the facts?

The Revenue of Ireland.

In 1852 the revenue of Ireland was 4½ millions.
In 1885 it was 8 millions.
An increase of 77 per cent.!

The Shipping of Ireland.

In 1852 the tonnage of shipping entering Irish ports was 5 millions.
In 1885 it was 13 millions.
An increase of 160 per cent.!

THE EXCISE DUTIES OF IRELAND.

In 1852 the Excise Duties of Ireland were 1½ millions.
In 1885 they had grown to 4½ millions.
An increase of 200 per cent.!

THE SAVINGS BANKS OF IRELAND.

In 1849 the amount in these was £1,200,000.
In 1887 it was £5,340,000.
An increase of 340 per cent.!

THE POST OFFICE SAVINGS BANKS.

(Being the popular banks with poorer depositors.)
In 1870 the amount was only £583,165.
In 1888 it had grown to £3,128,000.
An increase of 450 per cent. in eighteen years!

The same advance is evident in the material prosperity of the people.

HOUSING OF THE PEOPLE.

In 1841 there were 491,278 cabins of the poorest kind.
In 1881 there were but 40,665 of these.
A decrease of 92 per cent.!
In 1841 there were 304,264 houses of the better class.
In 1881 there were 488,968.
An increase of 60 per cent.!

EDUCATION.

In 1841, 28 per cent. of the population (young children excluded) could read and write.
In 1851, 33 per cent.
In 1861, 41 per cent.
In 1871, 49 per cent.
In 1881, 59 per cent.

NATIONAL SCHOOLS.

Year.	No. of Schools.	No. of Pupils.	Amount of Grant.
1837 ...	1,384 ...	169,548 ...	£50,000.
1885 ...	7,936 ...	1,075,604 ...	814,000.

The above figures show conclusively that the prosperity of Ireland has vastly increased since the Act of Union was passed.

3. The Consent of the Governed.

This argument is fallacious in assuming that the consent of the Irish alone should determine the Act of Union. But, taking it for what it is worth, there is one obvious answer, and it is this:—The Act of Union has now been in existence for eighty-eight years; it was undoubtedly passed with the consent of the people of Ireland. The dissatisfaction with it has not taken such intense form or lasted for as long a period as in the case of the Act of Union with Scotland in the last century. In the year 1790 it would have been no easy matter to draw up a list of representative Scotsmen of intelligence, worth, or patriotism, who did not hate the Act of Union. It is only 145 years since a Scottish army marched through England. It is only 100 years since Normandy and Brittany were at war with France. In any case Home Rulers propose to govern the Ulster settlement *in direct defiance of the consent of the governed.*

4. Coercion Acts Passed since 1800.

We have been told that there have been about 87 of these. To this there are two answers:—

(1) Grattan's Parliament passed 54 in eighteen years.

(2) An Irish Parliament, if now established, would be obliged either (*a*) to allow the Unionist community in Ulster to ignore its allegiance, or (*b*) to coerce that community.

It is no objection to the present state of things to urge that it necessitates "Coercion," unless it can be shown that under altered circumstances there will be no more "Coercion."

[For the complete facts of this branch of the subject, see Part III.]

E.—THAT A POLICY SIMILAR TO THAT OF HOME RULE HAS BEEN ELSEWHERE SUCCESSFUL.

THIS allegation, persistently made, is absolutely untrue. The whole assertion is made and based on a series of FALSE ANALOGIES, which require examination. Reference is perpetually made in the matter, (1) to certain European States where a system of Home Rule is supposed to exist, (2) to the colonial possessions of Great Britain, and (3) to the United States.

HOME RULE IN EUROPE.

It must always be remembered that there is no analogy whatever between Home Rule in countries where (like Great Britain and Ireland) the Executive is happily responsible to Parliament, and countries (like Austria-Hungary) where the Executive is responsible to the Sovereign alone. Austria and Hungary have separate Parliaments under one Emperor, who, however, by choosing his own Ministers, and keeping them in office, with or without the consent of either Parliament, secures Executive unity and stability. No one would dare to propose a constitution like this for Great Britain and Ireland. The argument is a sham—a Home Rule *false analogy*.

It may, however, be worth while to treat some of these cases in detail.

Germany.—We are often told that Germany has Imperial Unity, and twenty local Parliaments. To this it should be replied that this is the chief reason why Germany is still very nearly an absolute monarchy, and why the Reichstag, or National Parliament, has had so little power. There are as able public men in Germany as in England, but the parliamentary life of the nation is still in its infancy. It must be remembered, too, that in Germany, as also in Italy, the whole tendency of recent events has been to bind the various States more closely together in one great common nationality.

Austria-Hungary.—Hungary never had any connection with Germany, and was always quite independent of Austria in the earliest times. She had her own Constitution and Parliament for centuries, which were no more granted her by Austria than were such institutions granted to Austria by her. In 1848-9 she tried to gain *absolute separation.* When this failed, her parliamentary institutions were despotically set aside for a few years. The Hungarians are a different race from the Austrians, and have a different language; nor do they even belong, like Celts and Teutons, to a different branch of the Indo-European family.

Sweden, Norway.—In bygone days Norway was joined, not to Sweden, but to Denmark, with which latter she remained connected under her own Constitution from the fourteenth to the nineteenth century. At the present moment a large party exists in self-governing Norway which *wants to sever all connection* with Sweden. Here too comes a question of language. *A Norwegian cannot understand the speech of a Swede.*

Iceland, Denmark.—By history Iceland was an independent republic, joined to Norway in olden times. The 72,000 Icelanders are cut off entirely from Europe for five or six months in the year, and *they cannot understand Danish.* Is their case analogous to that of men from Aberdeen, Cork, Swansea, and London, who all understand each other perfectly?

Finland, Russia. — Russia seized Finland *in the present century*, and to wean the Finns from a previous political connection with Sweden, granted them a Diet. In fact the Finns have been systematically encouraged to cultivate their undoubted separate nationality in the hope of crushing out all sympathy with their Norse neighbours.

Switzerland.—Switzerland is the result of a process the very opposite to that Home Rulers wish to apply to the British Isles. Independent Commonwealths have there sought a closer union by means of Federation. Switzerland has four different languages—German, French, Italian, and Romansch.

Three of these are official in different states. In 1847 the question of State Rights involved Switzerland in Civil War!

HOME RULE IN THE COLONIES.

In reference to this the answer is almost self-evident. Ireland cannot be treated as if she were Canada or Australia. Leaving aside altogether the difference between a great continent 3,000 miles distant and a small island only 50, it must not be forgotten that, in several important respects, there is a necessary *separation* between Great Britain and her colonies. Most of the colonies can, if they like (and they *do* like), impose duties on British goods; while from not one of them has Great Britain the power to levy one farthing, even for war or Imperial defence. Moreover, it will hardly be disputed that if any of our great self-governing colonies chose to separate from us altogether, we should not go to war to prevent them. As it is, they can raise troops, levy militia and volunteers, interfere with vested interests, and do practically as they wish. Unless it is intended to put Ireland into a similar position, which has never been proposed, the self-governing colonies of Great Britain afford no argument for Irish Home Rule. It is another favourite Home Rule *false analogy*.

HOME RULE IN THE UNITED STATES.

When this is mentioned, it must be at once pointed out that the separate legislative assemblies of the different States are only possible, (1) because the Executive in the United States cannot be disturbed in office for four years, even by a Parliamentary vote; (2) because difficulties are obviated by a written Constitution, interpreted by a Supreme Court, which can veto laws passed by every Parliament; and (3) because, though there are many races, there are no national claims ever advanced in America by one State against another. In the United States Iowa or Massachusetts is not a separate State because it has, or is alleged to have, a separate nationality, which would be the case with Great Britain and Ireland. Here, again, is another *false analogy*.

It should be further recollected that in 1861 the Southern States insisted on their right, as separate commonwealths, to secede. In this they had the sympathy of Mr. Gladstone, who exultingly declared, against the late Mr. Bright and other prominent Liberals, "that Jefferson Davis had created an army and a navy, and was now creating a nation."

F.—THAT CERTAIN GRIEVANCES EXIST IN CONNECTION WITH THE LAND QUESTION.

WHAT these grievances may be is the subject discussed in Part II. of this book. It is, however, useful to bear in mind that if every alleged grievance in the Land Laws of Ireland be true, it only constitutes an argument for reforming these laws; *it is in no way an argument for setting up a Parliament in Dublin.*

In order to connect the Land Question of Ireland with Home Rule, it is necessary for Home Rulers to demonstrate that the United Parliament is unwilling or unable to remove unjust laws. How far this is true will be considered in Part II.

G.—THAT "COERCION" IS THE ONLY ALTERNATIVE TO HOME RULE.

THIS argument, or rather assertion, is the one most frequently heard by the Unionist speaker. Its truth must obviously depend on the facts of the case. If, for example, the only "Coercion" in Ireland be that, not of the Government, but of certain Nationalist bodies, the whole argument breaks down; if what is called "Coercion" be only the punishment of the law-breaker, the same result follows. It will, then, be necessary to discuss the facts of this subject at full length in Part III.

It must always be remembered by the Unionist speaker that "Coercion" is not an alternative to Home Rule, inasmuch as *the establishment of a Parliament in Dublin would have to be followed immediately by the "Coercion" of the Unionist population of Ireland.* The real alternative to Home Rule is the maintenance of the Union, coupled with the maintenance of law and order by the Imperial Government, supported by the United Parliament.

ADDITIONAL INFORMATION.

The leading arguments in favour of Home Rule have now been examined. There are, however, at least three other branches of the subject on which the speaker may require assistance. These are :—

1. Mr. Gladstone's Home Rule Bill of 1886.
2. The Separatist Objects of Irish Home Rulers.
3. The Impossibility of any Scheme of Home Rule.

1. MR. GLADSTONE'S BILL OF 1886.

THE following synopsis gives an accurate account of that measure :—

Section 1 established an Irish Legislature.

Section 2 gave the Legislature a general power to make laws, subject to restrictions in subsequent sections.

Section 3 excepted certain matters; among them—

Succession to the crown; peace and war; army, navy, and militia; foreign and colonial policy; treason; trade; post and telegraph; lighthouses; coinage.

Section 4 forbade the Irish Legislature to make any laws establishing a State religion; encroaching on certain religious and educational rights; impairing the existing rights of corporations; imposing Customs and Excise.

Section 5 gave the Queen the same prerogatives as in Great Britain.

Section 6 made the proposed Parliament quinquennial.

Section 7 vested the Executive Government in the Queen, represented by the Viceroy.

Section 8 provided for the use of Crown lands by the Irish Government.

Section 9 provided for two Orders, to deliberate and vote together, unless a majority of either Order should demand a separate vote, in which case the Orders were to vote separately.

Section 10.—The First Order was to consist of 103 members, 75 elective and 28 peerage members; the elective members to possess a property qualification of not less than £200 per annum. These elective members to be chosen by electors owning or occupying a house or tenement valued at not less than £25 per annum, and to hold office for ten years, half of them retiring at the end of each five years. The peerage members, elected by Irish peers, to hold office for life or thirty years, whichever period was shorter. These peerage and elective members to be utterly unaffected by any dissolution.

Section 11.—The Second Order to consist of 206 members, two to be returned by each of the 103 Irish constituencies.

Section 12 empowered the Irish Parliament to levy taxes, and established an Irish Consolidated Fund.

Section 13 provided for a yearly payment by Ireland to the Consolidated Fund of the. United Kingdom of £1,466,000 towards the National Debt; £1,666,000 towards the army and navy; £110,000 for Imperial Civil expenditure; £1,000,000 for constabulary and police.—Total £4,242,000.

Section 14 provided for the collection and application by the Imperial Treasury of Customs and Excise Duties paid in Ireland.

Section 15 provided for charges on the Irish Consolidated Fund; as, for example, for the salaries and pensions of judges.

Section 16 provided for the continued administration of "Irish Church" funds.

Section 17 transferred the receipt of moneys due to the Public Works Loan Commissioners, &c., to the Government of Ireland.

Section 18 provided that the Irish Legislature might appropriate out of Irish revenues additional sums of money to be paid into the Consolidated Fund of the United Kingdom in case of war.

Section 19 left the initiative in matters of taxation with the Crown. It provided that, notwithstanding Sections 3 and 4, an Irish Parliament in College Green might levy taxes for objects prohibited in those sections.

Section 20 provided that the judges of the Exchequer Division should remain under Imperial control.

Section 21 left the Dublin police under the control of the Lord-Lieutenant for two years, the Royal Irish Constabulary under the same control *as long as it existed*, and gave the Irish Legislature power to create other police forces under local authorities.

Section 22 reserved power over certain lands for Crown purposes, such as erecting magazines.

Section 23 provided that a veto on a Bill by the First Order should be in operation when the same measure was introduced a second time; such introduction, however, to take place after three years or a dissolution, "whichever period is longest."

Section 24 excluded all Irish peers and M.P.'s from the Imperial Parliament.

Section 25 provided for the decision of constitutional questions arising on the Act by a judicial committee of the English Privy Council.

Section 26 provided for the continuance of the Viceroyalty, the Viceroy to be paid out of the Consolidated Fund of the United Kingdom.

Section 27.—Future judges to be removable only on address from both Orders.

Section 28.—Present judges to have their rights and salaries protected.

Section 29.—Persons at present holding Civil Service appointments to be likewise protected.

Section 30 provided for existing pensions.

The foregoing were the leading provisions of the Bill of 1886. It will be observed that it utterly violated at least *three cherished principles of the great Liberal Party*:—

1. It proposed to set up the abominable doctrine of taxation without representation. (Sects. 13 and 24.)

2. It proposed to establish *sham* privileges, a *sham* House of Lords with *sham* qualifications and a *sham* veto. (Sects. 9 and 10.)

3. It proposed that on all questions arising between the two Parliaments—that is, between the people of Great Britain and the people of Ireland—the Imperial Parliament should no longer be supreme, but that the "Judicial Committee of the Privy Council" of England should be placed above Parliament. (Sect. 25.)

Finally, though it professed to be based on trust of the Irish people, it refused to trust them as to land, justice, or any of the important subjects mentioned in Sections 3 or 4.

SECTARIAN ENDOWMENT.

It did, however, allow the Irish Parliament to endow either the Roman Catholic Church or a Roman Catholic University, and the second subsection of Section 19 ran as follows:—

"Notwithstanding that the Irish Legislature is prohibited by this Act from making laws relating to certain subjects, that Legislature may, with the consent of Her Majesty in Council first obtained, appropriate any part of the Irish public revenue, or any tax, duty, or impost imposed by such Legislature for the purpose of, or in connection with, such subjects."

Under this section a Roman Catholic University could have been at once endowed and Protestants taxed for its support.

2. THE SEPARATIST OBJECTS OF IRISH HOME RULERS.

THE speaker who wishes to deal fully with this subject should provide himself with "As it was Said," a collection of extracts of speeches by Parnellite M.P.'s and others, published by the Irish Loyal and Patriotic Union.

The following are especially valuable as SAMPLE UTTERANCES :—

"And now, before I go, I will tell you an incident that happened in America. A gentleman came to the platform and handed me twenty-five dollars, saying, 'Here are five dollars for bread and twenty dollars for lead.'" MR. C. S. PARNELL, M.P., Dublin, April 29, 1880.

"None of us—whether we are in America or in Ireland, or wherever we may be—will be satisfied until we have destroyed the last link which keeps Ireland bound to England."

MR. C. S. PARNELL, M.P., Cincinnati, Feb. 3, 1880.

"I accept the Bill [a Franchise Bill] as far as it goes, but you need not think that it will have the effect of staying the agitation of a Separatist character which exists in Ireland ; for if you give us this Bill, or twenty more Bills of the same description, we will never cease from that agitation until we fully obtain our object."

MR. W. H. K. REDMOND, House of Commons,
on Franchise Bill of 1884.

"I will not mince my words, and I say that the one prevailing and unchangeable passion between England and Ireland is the passion of hate."

MR. T. SEXTON, M.P., Dublin, Oct. 14, 1881.

"The green flag of an independent Irish nation."

MR. W. O'BRIEN, M.P., Gorey, Aug. 23, 1885.

"We shall never accept, either expressly or implied, anything but the full right to manage our own affairs and make our land a nation; to secure for her, *free from outside control*, the right to shape her own destinies amongst the nations of the earth."

MR. C. S. PARNELL, M.P., Ennis, Nov. 3, 1885.

"We are working not simply for the removal of grievances. . . . The principle embodied in the Irish movement of to-day is just the same principle which was the soul of every Irish movement for the last seven centuries—the principle of rebellion against the rule of strangers; the principle which Owen Roe O'Neill vindicated at Benburb, which animated Tone and Fitzgerald, and to which Emmett sacrificed a stainless life."

MR. JOHN REDMOND, M.P., Chicago, Aug., 1886.

[N.B.—All the foregoing names are those of rebels, Tone being a rebel *when there was an Irish Parliament.*]

The following passages of more recent date are also remarkable as demonstrating the nonsense daily talked from Gladstonian platforms about the "*union of hearts*"—

"I hope there is civil war in every man's mind and heart, because, judging by the past, nothing but good can come out of the state of civil war." MR. JOHN O'CONNOR, M.P., at Ballylooby.
(See *Cork Herald*, Nat., Oct. 15, 1888.)

"Talk of meeting the enemy in arms! There is no man in Ireland would be more glad to do it than I would. But what is the use of talking about meeting the enemy in arms in the condition of things that prevail in this country." MR. JOHN DILLON, M.P., at Thurles, Oct. 25, 1888.
(See *Freeman's Journal*, Oct. 26.)

"I have never hesitated to express my admiration for the men of '67,* and I declare that our movement is in all its main principles, and the great issues at which it aims, the legitimate successor of that movement."

MR. JOHN DILLON, M.P., at Waterford, Dec. 8, 1888.
(See *Cork Herald*, Dec. 9.)

For further quotations from important speeches, *see* pp. 128, 129.

* The Fenian movement, the undoubted object of which was the entire separation of England and Ireland.

3. HOME RULE IMPRACTICABLE.

No more useful or important line of argument can be adopted by a speaker than that which is designed to show the absence of any scheme of Home Rule, and the impossibility of supplying any method which will ever recommend itself to the constituencies of the country.

A Scheme of Home Rule.

It cannot be too persistently pressed on public notice that Home Rule can never be passed by abstract resolutions, but only by the production of a thoroughly-matured scheme, in which all the details have been well considered.

One scheme of Home Rule—*and only one*—has yet been brought under the notice of the British Parliament and people by any politician. On April 8th, 1886, Mr. Gladstone introduced the famous Home Rule Bill of that year, which was rejected two months later (June 9th) by a majority of thirty. The details of that scheme have been already set forth at length. Here it is only noted that no other scheme has ever been mooted, so that there is none now before the country for examination. Either the scheme of 1886 is now dead, or it still survives; in the latter case all the objections already made to it possess their original potency.

There is, however, one obvious method by which all conceivable schemes of Home Rule can be classified and examined. Any possible method, any future Bill, must provide either for the *exclusion* from the Parliament still to sit at Westminster of the Irish representatives, or for their *retention*. When Ireland has been given a Parliament of her own, Irish members of Parliament must either be totally excluded from the British Parliament, or they must, subject perhaps to some restrictions, be retained there still. It is a useful task to examine these alternative methods of dealing with the question, and it must never be forgotten that, while Unionists object strenuously to the exclusion of the Irish members for the reasons presently stated, they protest with equal vigour against their retention. In fact, this is to them the cardinal point which shows the absurdity of the whole Home Rule movement, as they believe neither policy to be practicable.

Exclusion of the Irish Members.

The exclusion of the Irish representatives from the Imperial Parliament was a cardinal feature of the Home Rule Bill of 1886. (*See* Section 24 of that proposed measure.) It was also a leading argument in favour of Home Rule, as the following extract will show:—

Mr. John Morley on the Exclusion of the Irish Members.

"Do what you will with your old rules of procedure, you will not have restored the old British Parliament, you will not have made the British people master in its own House, until you have devised some scheme or other which will remove the Irish members from the British House of Commons."—Speech at Chelmsford, Jan. 7th, 1886.

From the several manifest absurdities connected with such a proposal, the following are the most obvious:—

1. If Irish members be excluded from the Parliament at Westminster, it follows that either the foreign policy of Great Britain and Ireland must be dictated entirely by English and Scotch voters, or that Ireland should be allowed to have a foreign policy of her own. The second of these alternatives is impossible; the first means the disenfranchisement of the inhabitants of Ireland on all questions of foreign policy.
2. If Irish members be excluded, it is equally evident that either Ireland will be deprived of all voice in the

control of an army and navy for which she will have to pay, or that she must be allowed to have an army and navy of her own. The second alternative is by universal consent impossible, the first is grossly unjust.

3. If Irish members be excluded, Ireland must be for ever without vote or voice in all questions arising out of the relations between the Mother Country and her colonies. These must be left entirely to England and Scotland.

4. If Irish members be excluded, Ireland must be for ever shut out from vote or voice in the management of Imperial trade, or Ireland must be permitted to pursue her own trade policy. The second alternative is, again, by universal consent impossible, the first grossly unjust.

5. If Irish members be excluded, it would follow that Ireland would be left no voice even in purely Irish trade. Parnellites have frequently reminded English audiences that separation between Ireland and England is impossible, because nineteen-twentieths of Irish trade at least is a cross-trade with Great Britain. Therefore under the Bill of 1886 it was found necessary to retain the management of *all* trade in a Parliament from which Irish opinion was rigidly excluded.

6. If Irish members be excluded, Ireland must either be free from all contribution to the Imperial revenue, or she must be taxed by a Parliament in which she has no representation. The former of these alternatives is obviously unjust, and so impossible that no one has dared to suggest it; the second is the policy of Lord North, whereby we lost our North American colonies one hundred and twenty years ago. The policies on this point of George III.'s Ministers in 1776 and of Mr. Gladstone in 1886 were identical.

TAXATION AND REPRESENTATION.

THE NORTH AMERICAN COLONIES.

IT is sometimes alleged by the more ignorant Home Rulers that Great Britain lost her North American colonies through a refusal to give them something in the nature of Home Rule. The contrary is the fact. Great Britain lost the North American colonies by trying to rule them on lines similar to those of Mr. Gladstone's Bill of 1886. The American colonies had Home Rule; they had their own Parliaments, and could tax themselves. They revolted, however, and were probably quite justified in so doing, because the Imperial Parliament, in which they had no members, sought to tax them further.

When the policy of "exclusion" is still further examined, it will be found at every point to reduce the Irish nation from a position of partnership in the freest Empire in the world to a position of uncompensated slavery. War might be declared against the United Kingdom a year after the passing of a Home Rule Bill such as that of 1886. Irish ports might be bombarded, Irish commerce might be destroyed, Irish soldiers might be slaughtered, but not a single Irishman would possess the inalienable right of a freeman to vote for or against the policy which brought about or conducted the war.

RETENTION OF THE IRISH MEMBERS.

To the policy thus criticised there is but one alternative, viz., the *retention* of the Irish representatives at Westminster. In this direction the policy of Home Rule seems to be gradually drifting.

MR. GLADSTONE ON THE RETENTION OF THE IRISH MEMBERS.

The famous and apparently contradictory utterances of Mr. Gladstone on this point will be of service :—

HOUSE OF COMMONS, April 8, 1886.

1. "Now I think it will be perfectly clear that if Ireland is to have a domestic Legislature, Irish peers and Irish representatives cannot come here to control English and Scotch affairs. That I understand to be admitted freely. I never heard of their urging the contrary, and I am inclined to believe it would be universally admitted. The one thing follows from the other. There cannot be a domestic Legislature in Ireland dealing with Irish affairs, and Irish peers and Irish representatives sitting in Parliament at Westminster to take part in English and Scotch affairs. My next question is, Is it practicable for Irish representatives to come here for the settlement, not of English and Scotch, but of Imperial affairs? In principle it would be very difficult, I think, to object to that proposition; but then its acceptance depends entirely upon our arriving at the conclusion that in this House we can draw, for practical purposes, a distinction between affairs which are Imperial and affairs which are not Imperial. It would not be difficult to say in principle that, as the Irish Legislature has nothing to do with Imperial concerns, let Irish members come here and vote on Imperial concerns. All depends on the practicability of the distinction. Well, sir, I have thought much, reasoned much, and inquired much with regard to that distinction. I had hoped it might be possible to draw a distinction, but I have arrived at the conclusion that it cannot be drawn. I believe it passes the wit of man. At any rate it passes, not my wit alone, but the wit of many with whom I have communicated."—(*Hansard.*)

SPEECH AT SINGLETON ABBEY, JUNE 5, 1887.

2. "I did not reject that opinion at all [*i.e.*, that the Irish members should be retained]; on the contrary, when Mr. Whitbread had given his view, I said there was great force in what he had said, but that I was not able to bind myself, much less my colleagues. . . . You will see that at the time we were perfectly open to consider a plan for the inclusion, if it should be found expedient, of the Irish members in the Westminster Parliament."—(*Daily News*, June 6th, 1887.)

SPEECH AT SIR WILFRID LAWSON'S ON JULY, 18TH, 1888.

3. "It [the retention of Irish members] is a matter on which I never had the slightest intention or disposition to interpose an objection. As to the mode of doing it, it is obvious that there are many—there may be a score—of modes of doing it. You may retain the present number of Irish representatives, or you may reduce it; you may elect Irish members to

Westminster directly, or you may elect them indirectly—that is, have them chosen by an intermediate body, such as the Irish representatives. You may allow them to sit in Parliament with the right to vote on all subjects, or you may give them a limited right to sit with power to vote on certain subjects. As to the practicability of making a plan, there is no question at all about it."—(*Daily News*, July 20th, 1888.)

LETTER TO REV. J. H. ROBINSON, BAPTIST MINISTER, DURING NORTH BUCKS ELECTION.

4. "At Singleton Abbey, in a reported and published speech, I long ago declared that the public sense appeared to be in favour of the retention of the Irish members, and that this being so, I was perfectly prepared to accede to the alteration."—(*Star*, October 1, 1889.)

Primâ facie, the policy of retention is impossible. Stated in all simplicity, it amounts to this :—On the Irish side of St. George's Channel a Parliament and Executive are to be established to manage the affairs of Ireland. Into the Parliament so established no English or Scotch member is to be permitted to enter, and Ireland is to "manage her own affairs." On the British side of St. George's Channel no reciprocity is to prevail. A Parliament is still to meet at Westminster, and among other business it is to transact the separate affairs of Great Britain. Into this Parliament, however, other than English and Scotch members will find their way. A certain number, if not all, of the Irish members will still come there, and in their hands will lie the power, after they are established by law in possession of their own Parliament and their own Ministry, to upset the Parliament or defeat the chosen Ministry of the people of England and Scotland. Whatever Home Rule means to Ireland, it means the ruin of the British Parliament.

THE DISTINCTION BETWEEN IMPERIAL AND LOCAL AFFAIRS.

It is often urged by Gladstonians, when they are successfully cornered in discussion, that of course Irish members in a new Parliament, after the establishment of Home Rule, would not be allowed to vote on English and Scotch affairs, but only on matters absolutely Imperial. It will be advisable to confront such persons with Mr. Gladstone's words of April 8th, 1886, just quoted. Whatever else that eminent statesman may have withdrawn, he has never withdrawn his assertion of the impossibility of drawing any distinction between Imperial and local affairs.

It should, however, be clearly pointed out that the retention of the Irish members to vote on only Imperial matters would absolutely destroy the Legislative Government of Great Britain. On a certain evening in the House of Commons—say, Monday—some local English or Scotch question is set down for discussion. No Irish members are admitted. The business of the House is conducted by a Government representing the majority of the members from England and Scotland. On Tuesday night an Imperial question is brought forward; 103 (or less) Irish members are now entitled to vote. In their hands—after they have received an unfettered Parliament of their own—the power has now been placed of turning out the Government which possesses the confidence of the people of England and Scotland. On Wednesday a local question arises, the Irish members withdraw, and so on. Permanence of Government becomes absolutely impossible anywhere except in Ireland, while the Parliamentary system of Great Britain is to be *dislocated.*

It must also be remembered that if the Irish members are to be retained in the Imperial Parliament, they must be retained either to vote on all questions, or on some. The examination of this next point, must invariably be pressed on the common sense of the electorate. The dilemma on which Home Rulers are impaled has never been more clearly stated than by the Marquis of Hartington at Stirling (October 4th, 1889.)

LORD HARTINGTON ON THE RETENTION OF THE IRISH MEMBERS.

"I suppose it will be conceded that if the Irish members remain in Parliament they must vote upon all questions or else provision will have to be made, and they will only be permitted to vote upon subjects considered Imperial, and they will not be permitted to vote upon subjects which relate to Scotland, England, or Wales. That, I think, is a proposition which cannot be denied. Supposing a separation has been made and Irish members are not allowed to vote upon English and Scotch subjects, we shall have Parliament constituted in two different ways for two different purposes. It is also equally clear that you may have two majorities in Parliament. A party which may be in a majority when only English and Scotch members are present, may be in a minority when Irish members come over to vote. The Home Secretary may be supported by a majority of English and Scotch members in his policy, the Foreign Secretary may be condemned by a majority of English, Scotch, and Irish members upon his foreign policy. You will have two majorities in the same Parliament. Is it not quite clear that if you have two majorities in Parliament, you must also have two Governments? You must have one Government for Imperial purposes, which will possess the confidence of Parliament when it is whole and complete, including the Irish members, and you must have another Government for purposes of internal policy, which will possess the confidence of the English, Scottish, and Welsh members, who alone will have anything to do with internal affairs. . . . But there is another alternative. You can retain the Irish members in Parliament and you can allow them to vote upon all subjects, and in reply to some observations which once before I made on this subject, a very able London paper, which has been the great champion of this form of Home Rule—a paper called the *Pall Mall Gazette*—said they entirely agreed with me. 'Of course,' they said, 'the Irish members, if they remain in Parliament, will remain for the purpose of voting upon all subjects.' Well, I should like to ask this assembly of Scotchmen, and I would ask every assembly of either Englishmen or Scotchmen, is it 'Of course'? When we have excluded ourselves from all control, from all authority over the internal affairs of Ireland, is it quite certain that the people of England and Scotland are going to allow the Irish members to come here and vote upon and settle their affairs? . . . The proposition appears to be indefensible as soon as it is stated. Ireland has a right, I admit—a right to equality of political treatment, but Ireland has no right, and I do not know who has ever claimed for Ireland the right, of political supremacy. And supremacy it would be if, having conceded to Irishmen the right to be masters in their own house, and the right to tell us that we had no title any longer to interfere in the settlement of the most important of their own internal questions, then they were to retain the right of coming over here and settling for us, perhaps contrary to the will and the wish of the majority of our representatives, the way in which we were to conduct our own internal affairs."

Federalism.

Some Home Rulers who see and appreciate these difficulties fancy that a way out of them may be discovered by the adoption of Federalism. This means the creation of, at least, five Parliaments—one for England, one for Ireland, one for Scotland, one for Wales, with an Imperial Parliament for Imperial affairs elected from all parts of the United Kingdom. This was understood to be the scheme of the late Mr. Isaac Butt, but has never yet been adopted by any responsible English statesman.

No attempt will be made in this Hand-book to discuss the question of Federalism at length. The following remarks will probably contain in them sufficient guidance for the speaker:—

1. Federalism is not yet the policy of either Mr. Parnell or Mr. Gladstone, or, indeed, of any considerable section of the Home Rule party.

2. Federalism destroys at once the main argument for Irish Home Rule, viz., that it is demanded by a majority of the Irish people. For if Home Rule is only the first step towards Federalism—if, in other words, Home Rule all round is a necessary logical result of Home Rule for Ireland—it is evident that it is just as much the business of Englishmen, Welshmen, and Scotchmen as of Irishmen, and therefore a question to be decided by the majority of the inhabitants of Great Britain and Ireland, and not by those of Ireland alone.

3. A federation of England, Ireland, Scotland and Wales could not work well, because England is far too large

and wealthy for her partners. In the American Union no one State exceeds the rest in total wealth and population. In Federated Britain, however, England would contain three-fourths of the population, and four-fifths of the wealth of the whole; and it is indeed doubtful if the members of the English Parliament, considering the past traditions of the body, would feel themselves at all inferior to those of the Imperial Assembly. In the English Parliament, too, the Queen would have Ministers who might be in opposition in the Imperial Parliament. In theory the former would be bound to give way, but is it certain they would do so in practice?

4. We are always told that if Ireland was dissatisfied with the new arrangement, and disloyal to the new Constitution we could then coerce her by conquest. Suppose England was restive, who would coerce or conquer her?

5. Federation has always been an intermediate stage in national growth, and never a final one. All over the world Federalism has invariably been a means of drawing together States at least semi-independent, with the result that either the bond has been tightened or dissolved altogether. The United States has grown out of Federated States of this kind, and the central power has been constantly growing till it is now recognised that *none of the States have the rights of nations.* They cannot secede, for example, and the entire strength of government is directed to the growth of a homogeneous nation.

6. In Great Britain in the past, everything has moved in the direction of building up *one* State. The Norman Conquest obliterated old sub-kingdoms, and England became homogeneous. Wales was next incorporated

(1536). Then came the union of the Scotch and English Crowns (1603) and Parliaments (1707). Lastly came the union with Ireland (1801). In the short space of eighty years wonders have been accomplished. The Irish language is dying out, means of inter-communication have multiplied a thousandfold, and assimilation is going on. It may be slow, but under the present system it is sure. But Federalism means to reverse all this, to substitute centrifugal for centripetal action, and to resolve the United Kingdom into its component parts.

7. Many people indulge in vague language to the effect that Home Rule is but a step in the direction of Federalising the British Empire. But Federalism of the British Empire, on which few men have yet got any positive ideas, and which our Colonies do not yet want, will not be simplified by first Federalising the United Kingdom, which is the nucleus of the Empire.

8. The difficulties of Federalism, and of the retention of the Irish members, cannot be better illustrated than in the words of one of the ablest of Home Rulers—Professor E. A. Freeman—spoken at Wells on October 4th, 1889, as follows:—

He was for Home Rule as he and they all understood it a few years ago, and as it was put forward in Mr. Gladstone's Bill. There had been latterly a great outcry about something different under the name of supporting Home Rule. He urged them, whatever they did, to do it with their eyes open, to know surely what the scheme was before saying yea or nay to it. They were for Home Rule for Ireland, but it did not follow that they wished to blot the name of England out altogether. There had been talk afloat which, if it meant anything, meant that England should be blotted out altogether. They had heard a vast deal about federation. He thought he knew what federation was. He had studied the subject all his life. They were told that the only path to Home Rule was through what was called federalism—that is, federation of the United Kingdom. Did they wish in granting Home Rule to Ireland to extinguish England, to wipe out themselves? That was not what Mr. Gladstone or Mr. Morley advocated. If Mr. Gladstone's Bill had passed and Home Rule had been given, the Irish members would have had a seat at Westminster no longer, and Mr. Gladstone adhered to that still. That was a question that involved a great deal more than appeared at first sight. There were several practical difficulties about it. If Irish members were to have votes in English and Scotch matters while English and Scotch members were not to have votes in Irish matters, granting Home Rule to Ireland would go a little further than that which both England and Ireland understood as Home Rule. To have a separate Parliament in Ireland, and have also Irish members in the Parliament of Great Britain, could have no meaning except it meant something like England being a dependency of Ireland; and they did not want to go quite so far as that. That would mean that the Parliament of Great Britain should no longer be a sovereign body, but should have something over it. . . . That was impossible. If the Parliament of England, which had done great things and made its name in the world for six hundred years, were to become a subordinate body, Englishmen would not submit to that. They could not make a federation of England, Ireland, Scotland, and Wales. It would be unfair. England would be so much greater than either of the others that they would have to submit to England. They did not want to submit to anybody else, and we did not want anybody to submit to us. If all wanted to be free and independent, the only way to fair federation would be to split up the Kingdom into smaller bodies by—what was said in jest, but in which there was truth in earnest—repealing the Union and restoring the Heptarchy. If the majority of the people thought England should cease to exist and should revive old divisions, let them say so with their eyes open. After having well considered and debated a point he was always open to conviction, and he might change his view even after winning the debate; but he would not take it as a consequence of Home Rule. That was his position; he was where he was several years back, where Mr. Gladstone and Mr. Morley were then and were now.

9. The entire subject of Federalism has received the fullest and most scientific investigation in the able work of Professor Dicey, "England's Case Against Home Rule."

HOME RULE NOT A FINAL SETTLEMENT.

Finally, that the Unionist party were perfectly correct when, in 1886, they warned the electorate that Gladstonian

Home Rule would never pacify the Irish party, may be clearly proved from the following comparatively recent utterances:—

"An ugly feeling was growing up among them that they had surrendered too easily to Mr. Gladstone for the kind of Home Rule to which they would be asked to agree."

MICHAEL DAVITT at Ballygarrett, Co. Wexford, Sept. 2, 1888.
(See *United Ireland*, Sept. 8.)

"They had established a right to a larger and wider scheme of Home Rule for Ireland than was originally proposed by Mr. Gladstone."

MR. T. D. SULLIVAN, M.P., at Dublin, Sept. 15, 1888.
(See *United Ireland*, Sept. 22.)

"*What is the truth underlying this movement? I beg leave to say that this movement to-day is the same in all its essentials as every movement which in the past history of Ireland has sought with one weapon or another to achieve the National rights of this land.* (Applause.) The truth underlying this movement to-day is precisely the same principle as that for which other generations have fought and died. *It is the principle that the sons of Ireland, and they alone, have the right to rule the destinies of Ireland.* (Hear, hear.) Gentlemen, I am prepared to maintain that more than that no Irish rebel leader in the past asked, and less than that I am here to maintain that no Irish leader of the present day can or ought to accept." (Applause.)

MR. JOHN EDWARD REDMOND, M.P., at Dublin.
(See *Freeman's Journal*, April 24, 1889.)

Even if Gladstonian Home Rule were carried, it could not have any finality. We should have civil war, or something like it, between the two Irish communities. We should have English soldiers, or Royal Constabulary, called upon to "coerce" the Ulster loyalists, and probably refusing to do so. We should have the landlords and manufacturing classes demanding help from Great Britain against the exactions of a Parnellite Parliament. If the Viceroy were to veto oppressive measures, there would at once be a new contest between him and his Ministers. The payment of contributions to the Imperial Exchequer would shortly be denounced as tribute unworthy of a free country. Each of the numberless restrictions placed on the action of the Dublin Parliament would, sooner or later, give rise to new agitation, and constant friction between the two Parliaments and Governments. In short, the evils of even a "dog-collar" Union are infinitely preferable to those of Home Rule.

Lord Derby on Finality.

Students of politics would do well to weigh the wise words of Lord Derby spoken in Liverpool in December, 1888:—

"If any man believes that in these two little islands there is room for four separate National Governments, with one Imperial Government over them all—five Cabinets and five Parliaments—and that all these Cabinets and Parliaments can continue to work together, he must be of an exceptionally sanguine disposition, or must possess the happy faculty, which some politicians have, of being able to shut their eyes very hard. You are sometimes told that there will be no peace till you have conceded Home Rule to Ireland. I answer, 'Will there be peace then?' Are any limits to be set to the powers of an Irish Parliament? If there are, those limits will supply material for fresh agitation. If there are not, how long will even two independent Legislatures go on side by side? Are we at Westminster to have power to overrule what is done in Dublin? If so, there is a grievance ready made. And if not, what link remains between the two countries? For the Executive in both must depend on its Parliament; and if the Parliaments diverge, how can the Executives agree?"

Part II.

THE IRISH LAND QUESTION.

AGRICULTURE, THE IRISH INDUSTRY.

IT must be carefully remembered that, important as agriculture is as an industry in Great Britain, it is incomparably more important in Ireland. This is so, simply because 35·6 per cent. of the whole male population of Ireland is engaged in agriculture, while in England and Wales the percentage is 10·4 and in Scotland 11·9.

The following tables (*the unproductive classes being omitted*) show the matter very clearly :—

Class.	England and Wales.	Scotland.	Ireland.
1. Professional	... 450,955	... 65,499	136,439
2. Domestic	... 258,508	... 25,292	34,068
3. Commercial	... 960,661	... 126,743	70,751
4. Industrial	... 4,795,178	... 675,964	428,578
5. Agricultural	... 1,318,344	... 215,215	902,010
Total	... 7,783,646	1,108,713	1,571,896

Reduced to percentages, the following results are obtained :—

Class.	England and Wales.	Scotland.	Ireland.
1. Professional ...	... 5·8	... 5·9	... 8·7
2. Domestic	... 3·4	... 2·2	... 2·1
3. Commercial ...	... 12·3	... 11·5	... 4·5
4. Industrial ...	... 61·6	... 61·	... 27·3
5. Agricultural ...	... 16·9	... 19·4	... 57·4
Total	... 100·0	100·0	100·0

The figures in these tables are taken from the census returns of 1881

This is the fundamental fact about the Land Question of Ireland.

Agriculture in Ireland mainly Pastoral.

A second important matter is the vast distinction between English and Irish agriculture as regards its quality.

	England.		Ireland.
Total acreage	32,597,398	...	20,328,753
Amount cultivated ...	25,000,000	...	15,500,000
Per cent.	76	...	76
Pasture and meadow ...	15,000,000	...	12,250,000
Per cent.	46	...	60
Crops	10,000,000	...	3,250,000
Per cent.	30	...	16

Small Holdings in Ireland.

A third matter of importance lies in the very small size of many holdings in Ireland. The following are the figures of the census of 1881 :—

	Number.		Per cent. of Total.
Holdings rated at or under £4	218,199	...	33·
,, ,, over £4 and not exceeding £10	196,934	...	29·8
,, ,, ,, £10 ,, ,, £15	77,712	...	11·7
,, ,, ,, £15 ,, ,, £30	92,870	...	14·1
,, ,, ,, £30 ,, ,, £50	37,679	...	5·7
,, ,, ,, £50 ,, ,, £100	24,424	...	3·7
,, ,, ,, £100	12,367	...	2·
Total ...	660,185		100·0

The following table gives the same information in a different shape. The figures are those of 1886 :—

	Number.		Per cent. of Total.
Holdings not over 1 acre in extent	47,800	...	8·3
,, over 1 acre and not over 5 acres	61,100	...	10·8
,, ,, 5 acres ,, ,, 15 ,, ...	157,600	...	27·9
,, ,, 15 ,, ,, ,, 30 ,, ...	134,800	...	23·8
,, ,, 30 ,, ...	162,800	...	29·2
Total ...	564,100	...	100·0

The difference between the two totals of 660,185 and 564,100 in the above tables arises from their being calculated on a different basis in the official returns. The former table gives the actual number of holdings; the latter excludes farms held by the same persons in adjoining town-lands, and therefore gives very nearly the number of tenants.

Thus it will be observed that one-third of the holdings of Ireland are rated at less than £4; that more than seven-eighths are rated under £30; that 19 per cent. are under 5 acres in extent, 47 per cent. under 15 acres, and over 70 per cent. under 30 acres.

The Irish Acre.

An Irish acre equals 1 acre 2 roods 19 perches Statute measure. It is to the Statute acre as 196 is to 121. Consequently, an Irish farmer who pays £1 per Irish acre for his holding (and there are many such cases) pays only 12s. 4d. per Statute acre.

Uncultivated Land.

Contrary to the popular impression, there is less uncultivated land in Ireland now than thirty years ago. The following figures are of interest :—

		Cultivated.		Uncultivated.	Total.
1851	...	15,303,780	...	5,023,984	20,327,764
1886	...	15,697,705	...	4,630,059	

The Hanging Gale.

It is important that this custom should be understood. It means that rent legally due on, say, March 31st, 1886, is not demanded nor payable by the custom of the estate for either six or twelve months later. Thus on the Vandeleur estate, at the time of the recent evictions, the rent was legally due up to March, 1888, but only asked for as due up to March, 1887, while by the custom of the estate the rent due in March, 1888, will not become payable till March, 1889. The custom is tantamount to allowing the tenants to be always one year in arrears. Unfortunately, if the landlord has to sue his tenants, he is legally obliged to sue for the full amount legally due, though in every case he is obviously willing to settle for the amount due by custom *or less*.

THE HISTORY OF THE IRISH LAND QUESTION.

It is impossible to understand anything about the Irish Land Question without some knowledge of its history. In connection with this the following facts are of importance :—

1. Up to the close of the last century Ireland was a purely pastoral country, breeding cattle, but growing no corn.
2. In 1650 the population was about 1,250,000; in 1750 it was about 2,500,000.
3. Towards the close of the eighteenth century a great economic change occurred, and Ireland was rapidly turned from a pastoral into a tillage country. This was due to the increasing population of England and the demand thence for food. The movement was accelerated by bounties on the exportation of grain, and every legislative encouragement.
4. As a consequence, the population began to increase very rapidly. In 1790 it was 4,000,000; in 1800 it was 5,000,000; in 1841 it was over 8,200,000.
5. This state of things was completely upset by the Famine, which led to a rapid decline in population and a speedy return from tillage to pasture.
6. While tillage has been decreasing in Ireland ever since the famine, pasture has been increasing correspondingly.

The Famine of 1846–47.

As most unfair attempts are made every day by the Nationalist Party to attribute the great Irish Famine to the Act of Union, as if the presence of Irish members in Westminster and their absence from Dublin could affect potato blight, and as utterly untrue statements have been published about the action of England at the time, and the action of Irish landlords, it may be advisable to give a few facts :—

1. £3,554,901 was given in 1847 to Ireland by England as a free gift. £3,968,239 were advanced as loans at the same time, making an aggregate of £7,523,140.

2. The following extract from "The Irish Crisis," by Sir C. E. Trevelyan (Sir G. O. Trevelyan's father), may prove interesting and instructive :—

   "This enterprise was in truth the grandest attempt ever made to grapple with famine over a whole country. Organised armies, amounting all together to some hundreds of thousands, had been rationed before ; but neither ancient nor modern history can furnish a parallel to the fact that upwards of three millions of persons were fed every day in the neighbourhood of their own homes by administrative arrangements emanating from, and controlled by, one central office."

3. The following quotation, refuting a current Nationalist fiction, is from the pen of the late A. M. Sullivan (Nationalist M.P.), in his work "New Ireland :"—

   "The bulk of the Irish landlords manfully did their best in that dread hour. No adequate tribute has ever been paid to the memory of those Irish landlords—and they were men of every party and creed—who perished martyrs to duty in that awful time ; who did not fly the plague-reeking workhouse, or fever-tainted court."

These references are important in view of the fact that Home Rule writers like Mrs. Josephine Butler and William Stephenson Gregg either ignore or minimise everything that was done.

HISTORY OF THE IRISH LAND LAWS PRIOR TO 1870.

PREVIOUS to 1870 the system of land tenure in Ireland was regulated by a large number of statutes passed at various times. Three of these, at least, require a passing notice, and are—

1. The Poor Relief Acts of 1838 and 1843.
2. The Act for the Relief of the Destitute Poor, 1848.
3. The Landlord and Tenant Act, 1860. (Deasy's Act.)

1. The Poor Relief Acts of 1838 and 1843 contained the following provisions :—

 (*a*) The landlord must pay HALF the Poor Rate if the Government valuation of a holding is £4 or upwards. (Poor Relief Act, 1843, Sect. 1.)

 (*b*) The landlord must pay the WHOLE Poor Rate if the Government valuation is under £4. (Poor Relief Acts, 1838, Sect. 74; 1849, Sect. 11.)

This is law in Ireland still, and it is important both in view of the fact that the Government valuation is under £4 in one-third of the total holdings of Ireland, and also because, in the case of every tenant, however wealthy, the landlord has to pay at least half the Poor Rate. Landlords have been compelled by Government to pay Rates amounting to thousands of pounds on rents which they never have received.

2. The Act for the protection and the relief of poor people evicted from their dwellings is a measure of which little is often remembered. It provides—

 (*a*) That before the execution of any Writ of Ejectment in Ireland, notice must be given to the Relieving Officer, who must provide shelter for the persons about to be evicted.

(*b*) That to pull down, unroof, or demolish any house, except so far as to enable the Sheriff to enter, while any tenant or any member of his family is within, is a misdemeanour.

It is well to recollect this Act, in view of recent Parnellite misrepresentations. At Glenbeigh some houses were unroofed and burned, but they were occupied, not by tenants, as the Parnellites tried to make people infer, but by trespassers.

3. The Act of 1860, commonly known as Deasy's Act, was an attempt to consolidate previous statutes and to amend the law. Like all preceding statutes, it proceeded on the assumption that the land was the exclusive property of the landlord, and that the tenant's interest in it was that of a person who had agreed to pay a certain remuneration for its use for a limited time. The following are the most important provisions :—

(*a*) The relation of landlord and tenant to be deemed to be founded on the express or implied contract of the parties, and not upon tenure and service. (Sect. 3.)

(*b*) No tenant can be evicted for non-payment of rent, UNLESS ONE YEAR'S RENT IS IN ARREARS. (Sect. 52.)

(*c*) A tenant can recover possession within six months after eviction by payment of the amount due, in which case the landlord is compelled to pay to the tenant the amount of any profit he could have made out of the land while the tenant was out of possession. (Sect. 70.)

TENANTS' IMPROVEMENTS.

One great and crying grievance, however, existed in Ireland until 1870. It must never be forgotten that, while in England *as a rule* the landlord has sunk money in the soil, has built the farmhouse, made the fences and the drains, in Ireland *as a rule* the reverse has been the case. On the majority of Irish holdings the tenants have built the houses, made the fences and the drains.

The evil of the old law obviously lay in the fact that, whereas an English tenant who gave up his holding lost nothing but the right of occupation, the Irish tenant in the majority of instances saw the valuable interest he had created in the holding, in the shape of permanent improvements, liable to confiscation at the hands of his landlord; for he might raise the rent to an impossible point, evict the defaulting tenant, and seize his improvements.

This scandal is every day placed before the notice of the electors of this country by Gladstonian speakers, who have never the honesty and candour to tell those whom they address that it has been absolutely abolished by the Imperial Parliament.

It took, however, many years to accomplish this. In 1835 Mr. Sharman Crawford moved for leave to bring in a Bill to amend the law by giving compensation for tenants' improvements. Unfortunately he had to struggle for twenty years without success, though in 1845 the Devon Commission (so called from its chairman, Lord Devon) reported after a two years' investigation strongly in favour of this measure of legislative protection for the tenantry.

At last in 1870 an important measure was introduced by Mr. Gladstone, with the three following objects:—

(*a*) To obtain for the tenants security of tenure by awarding them compensation for disturbance.

(*b*) To encourage and protect tenants' improvements by awarding compensation to the occupier who made them, whenever, either voluntarily or in consequence of eviction, he happened to leave his holding.

(*c*) To create a peasant proprietary by empowering the

Board of Works to advance money to tenants for the purchase of their holdings.

The following are the leading provisions of—

THE LANDLORD AND TENANT (IRELAND) ACT, 1870.

1. A YEARLY tenant who is disturbed in his holding by the act of the landlord for causes other than the non-payment of rent, and the Government valuation of whose holding does not exceed £100 per annum, must be paid by his landlord both—

   (*a*) FULL COMPENSATION FOR ALL IMPROVEMENTS made by himself or his predecessors, such as unexhausted manures, permanent buildings, and reclamation of waste lands; and

   (*b*) COMPENSATION FOR DISTURBANCE, a sum of money which may amount to seven years' rent. (Land Act, 1870, Sects. 1—3.)

Note.—This was law till 1881. Since then the power of disturbance by the landlord for anything else than non-payment of rent scarcely exists.

2. A yearly tenant *who is evicted by his landlord* for non-payment of rent must be paid—

   (*a*) FULL COMPENSATION FOR ALL IMPROVEMENTS, such as unexhausted manures, permanent buildings, and reclamation of waste land. (Sect. 4.)

   (*b*) In case his rent is under £15 he is entitled to a sum of money which may amount to seven years' rent, *as compensation for disturbance*, should the Court think the rent for non-payment of which he has been evicted an exorbitant one. (Sects. 3—9.)

3. Until the contrary is proved, all improvements are presumed to have been made by the tenants. (Sect. 5.)

4. The moment the landlord serves his notice to quit, the tenant can make his claim for compensation, *and cannot be evicted till the compensation be paid.* (Sects. 16 and 21.)

5. A yearly tenant, even when giving up his holding of his own free will, can compel his landlord either (*a*) to *compensate him for all improvements,* or (*b*) to let him sell his improvements to an incoming tenant. (Sect. 4.)

6. This Act of 1870 further provided that *in all new tenancies* the landlord must pay HALF the County or Grand Jury Cess if the valuation is £4 and upwards, and ALL the County or Grand Jury Cess if the valuation is under £4. (Sect. 65, 66.)

It will be observed, therefore, that under this Act all tenants whose holdings were valued at £100 and under—*i.e.*, 98 per cent.—received FULL COMPENSATION FOR IMPROVEMENTS; and all tenants valued at less than £15—*i.e.*, 74 per cent.—or all the poorer tenantry, received the right of COMPENSATION FOR DISTURBANCE.

It is necessary for the Unionist speaker to be on his guard against the amazing amount of fiction talked on this matter by the Parnellites. They sometimes give *alleged* instances of poor tenants who have been evicted and got no compensation; in every one of these cases it will be found either—

(*a*) That there were no permanent improvements at all;

(*b*) That the landlord paid for them at the time by giving a large reduction of rent till the price was paid; or

(*c*) That the amount of rent owed extinguished the value of the improvements.

(*d*) That the tenant, instead of using his legal rights,

resolved to fight against the law, refusing to leave and take compensation.

How Compensation may be Lost.

Of course a tenant may lose his compensation money by getting heavily into his landlord's debt, and the Parnellites call this one of their grievances. Suppose A B, a tenant, owes C D, his landlord, four years' rent at £40 per annum—that is, £160—but A B has made permanent improvements to the extent of £100, how does the case stand? In the eye of the law, as well as in common justice, the landlord owes the tenant £100 for improvements, and the tenant owes the landlord £160 for rent. Parnellites like Mr. J. J. Clancy, M.P., are every day to be found pretending that, whether the landlord gets his £160 or not, he is to give £100 to the tenant. This is a fitting illustration of Parnellite morality. It must be remembered that every newspaper story of a poor tenant evicted for £30 or £40 of rent, and thereby losing £300- or £400-worth of improvements, IS AN ABSOLUTE UNTRUTH; it is an attempt to describe *an outrageous impossibility*.

Amount of Compensation Paid.

As a matter of fact, £160,035 was paid to tenants as compensation under this Act between 1870 and 1881, and a large sum since the latter date.

Ulster Tenant-Right Custom.

It should be remembered that long prior to the Act of 1870 the Ulster tenantry possessed both security of tenure and compensation for improvements; this they did not by possess by law, but simply by custom, under which the sum paid to outgoing tenants included both compensation for improvements and the price of goodwill. The process of the Act of 1870 was therefore to legalise the Ulster custom. This was done in Section 1. Section 2 legalised any similar customs in other parts of Ireland. Sections 3 and 4 affected the tenantry in other parts of Ireland, and to them the privileges already enumerated were very properly given.

THE BRIGHT CLAUSES.

These embodied the first serious attempt made to make the occupier the owner of his holding. In Sections 32—47 of the Act of 1870 it was provided that when the landlord and tenant agreed for the sale of a holding, either of them might apply to the Commissioners of Public Works, and the tenant might obtain an advance of two-thirds of the value of the holding, the advance to be repaid by annuities at the rate of £5 for every £100 lent, payment extending over thirty-five years.

Tenants who purchased under this Act have since been enabled to extend the time of payment, and to reduce the rate to £4 per cent.; but the entire question of Land Purchase will be dealt with more fully under the Act of 1885.

RACK-RENTS.

There are some few matters deserving consideration and demanding explanation before one proceeds to deal with the second great legislative measure passed on behalf of the Irish tenant-farmer. Foremost among these is the current Parnellite assertion that Irish tenants were cruelly "rack-rented" by their landlords.

In proof of this assertion three arguments are adduced:—

1. The rents are stated to have been far over the Government or "Griffith's" valuation.

2. It is alleged that large increases in rent were made by landlords during recent years.

3. The reductions granted by the Land Commissioners under the Act of 1881 have been supposed to indicate previous extortion.

The third of these arguments is examined on page 84. Some examination of the others is necessary before proceeding to the Land Act of 1881.

With regard to the word "RACK-RENTS," it may, however, be pointed out that the whole case has been obscured by a false meaning imported into the word by Parnellite orators, and largely accepted by ignorant people among their auditors, who seem to fancy that a "rack-rent" means something "extorted," as if by the "rack," from tenants. "Rack-rent" is simply a legal term denoting a particular class of rent paid by ALL yearly tenants, and is *applicable to the money paid by the lowest-rented tenant in Ireland, as well as to that paid by the highest-rented.*

THE GOVERNMENT OR GRIFFITH'S VALUATION.

This is the Government or Ordnance valuation of Ireland, but it has no reference whatever to the question of rent. It bears its name from Sir Richard Griffith, under whose direction it was made. The valuation of Ireland is at present regulated chiefly by an Act passed in 1852 and subsequently amended; and the valuation was based entirely on the prices of the day, which, as will be presently seen, bore no reference to those of the present time.

Sir R. Griffith's opinion of his own valuation, which was made for rating purposes, was "that if one-third be added the result will give very nearly the full rent-value of the land."

In addition to this, it should be remembered that the valuation given in the Government Act was not made simultaneously in all parts of Ireland. Ulster was valued when prices were fairly high; Munster, under an Act of 1846, during or just after the Famine, when prices were extremely low and agriculture depressed. In short, the Government valuation, in consequence of its inequalities and variations, is absolutely useless as a standard.

Old Increases of Rent.

It is an undoubted fact that between 1850 and 1875 it was not uncommon for an Irish landlord to raise the rent of his tenantry. It is not difficult to bring forward instances in which this was done; but, as usual, the Parnellites give a totally false impression of the facts. (1) They always choose to assume that any increase of rent is a grossly arbitrary act; (2) they also assume that whenever they find an increase of rent on an estate, this must have been a case in which the landlord raised the rent on his unfortunate tenants' improvements.

Both these assumptions are utterly untrue, and utterly unsupported by evidence; but, as they deceive unthinking persons, they deserve a separate examination.

1. Every case of an increase in rent between 1850 and 1875 is fully justified by a matter which is always sedulously concealed from the public—namely, that during those years there was an enormous rise in prices. Rents were justly raised then for economic reasons. In Ireland, or in any other country, you may regulate the amount of rent by one or other of two methods: you may either have an immovable rent, or a sliding rent, varying according to the rise or fall in the price of agricultural produce. It is now universally considered just that a farmer's rent should vary according to prices. Parliament has interfered to lower Irish rents because prices have gone down. If this is just, it is equally just to raise rents if prices go up. The Parnellite motto is to say to the landlord, "Heads I win, and tails you lose." Rents are to fall now, because of prices, but they never are to rise when prices are high. The following table gives the average market prices of farm-produce in Ireland in the years mentioned :—

	Minimal Prices.			Maximal Prices.		
	1850.	1875.	Increase per cent.	1850.	1875.	Increase per cent.
Two-year-old cattle	£4 0 0	£10 0 0	150	£9 0 0	£12 0 0	33
One-year-old ,,	1 5 0	7 0 0	460	5 0 0	9 0 0	80
Milch cows	6 0 0	16 0 0	166	12 0 0	24 0 0	100
Lambs	0 14 0	1 5 0	78	1 3 0	2 2 0	82
Beef, per cwt.	1 10 0	3 10 0	133	2 8 0	4 7 6	83
Mutton ,,	1 17 4	3 5 4	75	2 16 0	4 4 0	50
Pork ,,	1 10 0	2 18 0	93	2 2 0	3 0 0	42
Wheat ,,	0 8 0	0 9 5	17	0 10 0	0 10 0	=
Oats ,,	0 5 10	0 8 2	40	0 6 10	0 8 2	19
Barley ,,	0 5 3	0 8 8	65	0 6 9	0 8 8	28
Flax ,,	2 0 0	3 0 0	50	3 10 0	4 8 0	25
Hay ,,	0 2 0	0 5 6	175	0 2 10	0 6 0	111
Straw ,,	0 0 8	0 2 6	275	0 1 4	0 4 0	200
Potatoes ,,	0 4 6	0 3 0	D.–33	0 5 0	0 4 0	D.–20
Butter ,,	2 12 0	5 15 0	121	3 14 0	7 0 0	89
Eggs, per 120	0 4 6	0 7 3	61	0 4 8	0 9 0	92
Wool, per lb.	0 0 10	0 1 5	70	0 1 1½	0 1 8	48

These prices are taken from the returns published in the Appendix to the Report of the Royal (Cowper) Commission, 1887.*

On a later page a further list of prices with reference to the subsequent fall will be given, but the present extraordinary table is amply sufficient to prove the absolute justice of an increase in rent, when the market value of land must have been well-nigh doubled.

It may be well to apply the facts of this table to some of the Parnellite cases. Mr. Waddy, Q.C., has, for example, told some stories which have received wide circulation throughout the country, and which seem extraordinary until they are explained.

One is the case of a man called Tuohy, who, shortly after the Famine, when the price of land was unnaturally depressed, got a farm for £25 yearly rent. By 1870 his rent had been raised to £56. This is supposed to have been unjust; in reality, it was an eminently just proceeding.

* See also page 86.

In 1852 Tuohy was paying, *willingly*, £25 rent. We may assume the value of the gross produce in the farm could not have been less than £70; this left Tuohy £45 to live on. In 1870, however, with the increased prices, he must have got from the farm at least £120; take his 1870 rent, £56, from that total, and he had at least £64 to live on. Under the high rent he was, then, at least 40 per cent. better off than under the low rent of low prices.

2. With regard to the second point of the Parnellites—that rents were raised "on" or "because of" the tenants' improvements—that is absolutely without proof. As an assertion, it is mere guess-work; it has been adopted, however, by people who did not know, or who chose to forget, the rise in prices, and who therefore were at a loss for an explanation for the rise in rent.

It should also be recollected that in 9 cases out of 10 the rent has been raised because fresh land has been added. Thus in November, 1885, the *Freeman's Journal* attacked the Duke of Abercorn for raising his rents; but it was proved on oath in Court that in every case the holding had been enlarged.

That holdings in Ireland have been enormously enlarged is obvious, since there is more land in cultivation now than in 1851 (*see* p. 66), while the population is less by 30 per cent., and the total number of holdings by 20 per cent.

Causes of the Land Act of 1881.

The Act of 1870 was passed at a time of high prices. A sudden fall unfortunately succeeded, and the distress which ensued was aggravated by bad harvests and general depression of trade. It is worth while recollecting that the Land League was founded in 1879, and that at the conference summoned by that body, and held in Dublin in April, 1880, resolutions were carried in favour of a large scheme of Land Purchase, under which the landlords would receive twenty years' purchase of the Government valuation of their holdings.

In 1881 Mr. Gladstone's Government brought in the Land Law (Ireland) Act. Its object was, (1) the fixing of fair rents, (2) security of tenure, (3) free sale of tenancies, and (4) increased facilities for purchase. In popular language it conferred on the Irish tenants "the three F's"—Fair Rent, Fixity of Tenure, and Free Sale.

It is to be remembered that the prevalent distress in Ireland consequent on the fall in agricultural prices was the sole reason for the introduction of this measure. It is often pretended by the Parnellites that landlord oppression made it necessary. In view of such statements it is well to recall the following words :—

Mr. Gladstone on the Irish Landlords (1881).

"Well, Sir, neither, I am bound to say, should we think it just to propose legislation on this great matter on the ground, whether expressed or implied, of general misconduct on the part of the landlords of Ireland. On the contrary, as a rule they have stood their trial and have as a rule been acquitted. The report of the Bessborough Commission, which certainly is not deficient in its popular sympathies, in its tenth paragraph declares that the greatest credit is due to the Irish landlords for not exacting all that they are by law entitled to exact; and it likewise points out that if they had exacted all they were entitled to, they would have been guilty of injustice; they would have appropriated their tenants' labours in the soil. Again, I find in the ninth paragraph a remarkable statement :—'It was unusual to exact what in England would have been considered a full or fair commercial rent. Such a rent over many of the larger estates, the owners of which were resident, and took an interest in the welfare of their tenants, it has never been the custom to demand. The custom has been largely followed, and is to the present day the rule rather than the exception in Ireland.'"—Speech in House of Commons on introduction of Land Act (*Hansard*).

THE LAND LAW (IRELAND) ACT, 1881.

This Act—the largest and most important of all those passed for Irish agriculture—gave three privileges to the tenant-farmers of Ireland, popularly known as "the three F's," namely, FIXITY OF TENURE, FAIR RENT, and FREE SALE, while it gave increased facilities for purchase. It will be well to discuss these subjects separately.

1. By FIXITY OF TENURE the tenant was enabled to remain in possession of his land FOR EVER, subject to periodical revision of his rent. (Sect. 8.)

2. Under FAIR RENT yearly tenants may apply to the Land Commission Court (the overwhelming majority of the judges of which were appointed by Mr. Gladstone) to fix the fair rent of his holding. This application* is referred to three persons, one of whom is a lawyer, while the other two, who are agriculturists, inspect and value the farm. THIS RENT CAN NEVER BE RAISED AGAIN BY THE LANDLORD. (Sect. 8.)

It is important to bear in mind that if a tenant has not had a fair rent fixed, and his landlord proceeds to evict him for non-payment of rent, he can apply to the Court to fix the fair rent; and, meantime, the eviction proceedings will be restrained by the Court. (Sect. 13.)

3. FREE SALE.—By this provision every yearly tenant, whether he had a fair rent fixed or not, MAY SELL HIS TENANCY to the highest bidder whenever he desires to leave (Sect. 1); while even if a tenant be evicted he has the right either to redeem *within six months*, or to SELL HIS TENANCY WITHIN THE SAME PERIOD TO A PURCHASER, WHO CAN LIKEWISE REDEEM, and thus acquire all the privileges of the tenant. (Land Act, 1881, Sect. 13.)

A further explanation of the working of these privileges will be found in the succeeding paragraphs:—

* It is important to remember that by the Act of 1887, the fair rent dates not from the decision of the Court, but from the application of the tenant, see p. 98.

Fixity of Tenure.

Fixity of tenure is consequent on having a fair rent fixed. The tenant then is practically turned into a leaseholder for fifteen years, at the end of which term he is started, at a revised rent, for a further period of fifteen years. During this period the landlord cannot add a farthing to his rent, though landlords are frequently abused for not making large abatements in it.

Fair Rent.

Under the Fair Rent provisions of the Act of 1881, Courts have gone and go yearly into every one of the thirty-two counties of Ireland, fixing "fair rents" as between landlord and tenant. Down to August, 1888, fair rents were fixed in 204,840 holdings, with a total acreage of 5,758,777 acres. The old rents were £3,851,891, an average of less than 13s. 6d. an acre. The judicial rents are £3,093,807, or less than 10s. 9d. an acre!

Misrepresentations about Fair Rent.

Utterly apart from the usual Parnellite method of omitting all reference to the Legislation of 1881, there are three distinct Parnellite misrepresentations against which speakers should be warned. These misrepresentations are as follows:—

1. Of pretending that hosts of tenants are excluded by one means or another from the operation of the Act.

2. Of pretending that arrears of rent prevent the fixing of a fair rent.

3. Of pretending that the reductions of rents made already prove antecedent rack-renting by the landlords.

It will be necessary to deal separately with these.

Exclusion of Tenants.

It is absolutely certain that certain tenants are excluded from the benefits of this Act.

These exceptions are—

1. Less than 2 per cent., being the larger tenants of purely pastoral holdings.
2. The leaseholders (since, however, admitted; *see* Act of 1887).
3. Future tenants, who are left to make their own bargain. (Why not?)
4. Tenants of pasture lettings, *who are non-resident.* (Why should Parliament treat the butcher as a farmer, and root him in the soil?)

Some other very small exceptions exist, all of them quite easy of explanation on equitable grounds. As a matter of fact, the Act applies to every *bonâ-fide* yearly agricultural tenant. In his work on the Land Law (Ireland) Act, p. 40, Mr. T. M. Healy, M.P., having enumerated the exceptions, says, "On the whole it will be seen that *none of the tenant-farming class,* whom the Act was passed to benefit, are affected by these various exclusions."

Sometimes the Parnellites point to the 565,000 holdings in Ireland, and then to the fact that only 100,000 fair rents have been fixed in Court, as indicating the limited scope of the Act.

This is altogether absurd, for as many more have been fixed out of Court; in addition to which, it should be remembered that *thousands of tenants have declined to go into Court,* because, (*a*) they believed their present rents to be fair, or (*b*) were satisfied with the abatements made by their landlord, or (*c*) were induced by the National League not to avail themselves of their legal privileges. The necessary cost to a tenant of getting a fair rent fixed amounts to FIFTEENPENCE, and for that sum many thousand rents have been judicially fixed.

ARREARS AND FAIR RENT.

It must be carefully noted that the existence of arrears creates *no statutory obstacle whatever, nor any difficulty in procedure* to a tenant desirous of applying to have a fair rent fixed. [For further remarks on Arrears, *see* p. 91.]

A JUDICIAL REDUCTION NO PROOF OF PREVIOUS EXTORTION.

We are now brought face to face with the most common misrepresentation of the Nationalist Party. It will be observed that while frequently impeaching the conduct of the Land Commissioners—as, indeed, of all officials—they also frequently appeal to the decisions of these same Commissioners as giving distinct proof that the landlords of Ireland have in the past "rack-rented" their tenants grievously.

This is frequently done by the citation of some decisions of the Land Commission summarised in the following form :—

Landlord A. B.

Name of Tenant.	Old Rent.	New Rent.	Reduction per cent.
C. D.	£40 0 0 ...	£32 0 0 ...	20
E. F.	33 6 8 ...	25 0 0 ...	25
G. H. ...	50 0 0 ...	34 0 0	32
I. J. ...	7 10 0 ...	4 0 0 ...	$46\frac{2}{3}$

These are fairly typical cases, especially of late years, and they are every day triumphantly cited by the Separatist press as proofs of landlord malpractices.

Yet nothing can be clearer than that they prove nothing whatever of the kind ; and for the following reasons :—

1. They leave out of sight the fact that these rents *were perfectly fair* when they were fixed in the days of high prices. The Land Commission never determined

that *they* WERE *unfair rents in the past;* it has only determined that, in consequence of the fall in prices, *they* ARE *unfair* at present.

2. It is also forgotten that the rents in the first column do not represent what the landlords have been demanding from their tenants, they only represent the old contract rents fixed in the day of high prices; but *in thousands of cases* the landlord has voluntarily been making abatements equal to, or even larger than, those granted by the Land Commission.

When, therefore, a speaker is confronted with cases of the kind described, he must point out that the first column truly states the original contract rents, but that no column gives any information about the amount of the rent which the landlord has been demanding, which very frequently has been at least 25 per cent. less than that given in the first column. Cases have occurred, as at Glenbeigh and on the Vandeleur estate, where there has been loud talk about rack-rented tenants who did not pay a farthing for years.

In reply to this an attempt may be made by the Parnellites to point to the judgments sometimes obtained by landlords against their tenants. Thus they will say A. B. was rented at £25 per annum. He was three years in arrears. His landlord evicted him for £75, proving thereby that no abatement was made.

This argument, however, is utterly misleading, inasmuch as a man may be evicted really on account of his unwillingness to pay *anything*, but technically on account of a full demand. Thus a tenant may owe his landlord £100. The landlord may express his willingness to take £20, *and such is a very common case.* If the tenant will pay nothing, the landlord, like any other creditor, will naturally sue for the full amount legally due, otherwise he might legally lose everything.

In addition to what has been said, it must be remembered that just as prices rose in Ireland between 1850 and 1872, so they have been falling since. This being so, *if the old contract rents were perfectly fair when made*, the Land Commissioners were bound to make important reductions. Let us see what the fall in prices was. We shall give a similar table to that already printed on p. 78, with which this may be well compared :—

	Minimal Prices.			Maximal Prices.		
	1875.	1885.	Decrease per cent.	1875.	1885	Decrease per cent.
Two-year-old cattle	£10 0 0	£7 0 0	−30	£12 0 0	£13 0 0	1+9
One-year-old ,,	7 0 0	4 0 0	−42	9 0 0	8 10 0	−6
Milch cows	16 0 0	11 0 0	−32	24 0 0	20 0 0	−17
Lambs	1 5 0	0 18 0	−28	2 2 0	2 10 0	1+19
Beef, per cwt.	3 10 0	2 0 0	−43	4 7 6	3 10 0	−20
Mutton ,,	3 5 4	2 0 10	−38	4 4 0	4 8 8	1+5
Pork ,,	2 18 0	1 12 0	−45	3 0 0	3 0 0	=
Wheat ,,	0 9 5	0 6 9	−29	0 10 0	0 10 2	1+2
Oats ,,	0 8 2	0 6 0	−27	0 8 2	0 10 0	1+22
Barley ,,	0 8 8	0 6 7	−24	0 8 8	0 8 3	−5
Flax ,,	3 0 0	2 2 0	−30	4 8 0	3 8 0	−23
Hay ,,	0 5 6	0 1 8	−70	0 6 0	0 5 6	−9
Straw ,,	0 2 6	0 2 0	−20	0 4 0	0 4 0	=
Potatoes ,,	0 3 0	0 1 6	−50	0 4 0	0 3 8	−9
Butter ,,	5 15 0	2 14 0	−53	7 0 0	6 16 0	−3
Eggs, per 120	0 7 3	0 5 9	−21	0 9 0	0 11 3	1+25
Wool, per lb.	0 1 5	0 0 7½	−57	0 1 8	0 0 10½	−48

There can be no doubt that the average fall in prices may be estimated as between 1874 and 1885 as not less than between 25 and 30 per cent. In all propriety, then, rents should have been reduced that much by the Land Commission *if the old rents were fair rents.*

How much, however, were the rents reduced? The following list shows the average reductions made :—

Average Reductions made in the Old Rent.

For the year ending August, 1882	... ...	20·5 per cent.
,, ,, ,, 1883	... ...	19·5 ,, ,,
,, ,, ,, 1884	... ...	18·7 ,, ,,
,, ,, ,, 1885	... ...	18·1 ,, ,,
,, ,, ,, 1886	... ...	24·1 ,, ,,

[For further subsequent reductions, see Land Act of 1887.]

The above table is quite sufficient to demonstrate that judged by the decisions of the Land Commission, to which the Parnellites are never tired of appealing, the statement that Irish landlords as a class have "rack-rented" their tenantry is an outrageous calumny. The Commission has never done more than reduce rents in proportion to the acknowledged fall in prices.

REDUCTIONS VARY WITH SIZE OF HOLDING.

Parnellites, however, occasionally attempt to prove individual cases of hardship by citing specimen cases of larger reductions than the average. They point to a few cases where reductions of 40, 50, 60, 70 per cent., or even more, are given. *All such cases are absolutely illusory*, though their existence is a pitfall to the ignorant. In this case everything depends on the size of the holding, for the following reason :—

It has been the invariable practice of the Irish Land Commission to fix such a rent for a holding as will enable the tenant to live and pay his way. It is quite obvious that, if this is to be done, a fall in prices of 30 per cent. will necessitate a larger reduction on a small holding than on a large one. Let us illustrate this :—

James Finucane (shall we say?) pays £100 rent for 75 acres of good land. When times are good he makes £250 gross profit out of the land. He pays £100 rent, and lives on £150. Prices fall 30 per cent. ; he then only makes £175. If his rent is reduced 30 per cent., he pays £70, and has £105 to live on. In other words, the loss on the farm is 30 per cent. He loses 30 per cent., and so does his landlord—a not inequitable arrangement.

Patrick Dowling (shall we say ?) is a small farmer; he pays £2 rent for 2 acres of middling land. When times are good he makes £20 gross profit out of the land, perhaps by the sale of cattle. Of course he has his own potatoes, which probably he does not sell. He pays £2 and has £18 for clothing and stock. Prices fall 30 per cent.; then he makes only £14 out of the land. If his rent is reduced to £1 8s. (that is, 30 per cent.), he is left with a sum quite inadequate to clothe himself and his children, and it becomes perfectly clear that a Commission fixing rents on the "live and thrive" principle will be obliged to reduce his rent to almost nothing.

It is obvious to every thinking man that while on this principle a large farmer may get a reduction of 15 or 20 per cent., larger reductions have to be given to poor cottiers; and no list of statements is reliable which ignores this fact.*

Free Sale.

The following illustrations of what can be done under Free Sale—which recognises the valuable interest of the tenant in his holding—have occurred since the introduction of Mr. Gladstone's Home Rule Bill. They are selected from different parts of Ireland, prosperous and poor :—

Name of Landlord.	Name of Tenant.	County.	Rent.	Price obtain'd by Tenant for Interest.	No. of Years' Purchase.
Lord Massereene	William Anderson	Antrim	£30 0 0	£730 0 0	25
"	Repr. of John Swann	"	4 4 0	170 0 0	40
Trustees of late T. Conolly	Hugh Walsh	Donegal	4 2 6	130 0 0	31½
" "	Condy Bradbane	"	3 14 0	140 0 0	38
Duke of Devonshire	James Sullivan	Cork	18 0 0	217 0 0	14
S. M. Hussey	Edmond Walsh	Kerry	10 2 0	100 0 0	9½
Sir S. Hayes, Bart.	Mrs. Long	Donegal	18 0 0	270 0 0	15
—	Repr. of Anne Johnston	Monaghan.	22 10 6	525 0 0	23
Sir Augustus Stewart	James Black	Donegal	12 0 0	400 0 0	33
— Gun, Esq.	B. Dooling	Kerry	17 10 0	208 0 0	12

* It may be urged that there are serious objections in theory to such a method of dealing with rents as that of giving larger reductions to one class than to another. We are not concerned with that question, but with the fact that it is done, and has to be done, by the Land Commission.

It should be remembered that, despite the opposition of the League, *about* 300 *such sales take place in Ireland annually.* By them the outgoing tenant is enabled to pocket money representing the interest in his holding, while the incoming tenant testifies his confidence that *the rent is perfectly fair*, inasmuch as he is quite willing to pay down a large sum of money to be allowed possession of the farm subject to the rent.

The following table gives the number of sales and number of years' purchase for the tenant's interest during the first four years of the operation of the Land Act of 1881 :—*

Number of cases in which the price paid represented an equivalent to—	Ulster.	Leinster.	Munster.	Connght.	Ireland.
10 years' purchase and under	253	121	133	63	570
Over 10 and under 20 years'	275	49	71	55	450
,, 20 ,, ,, 30 ,,	81	7	25	9	122
,, 30 years' purchase	43	3	10	2	58
	652	180	239	129	1,200

It will be observed that more than half the sales occurred in the province of Ulster.

For this fact there could only be four possible reasons :—

1. Some difference in the law, operating in favour of Ulster and against the other provinces.
2. That in Leinster, Munster, and Connaught the tenants' interest was of less value than in Ulster, probably because the tenants' improvements, &c., were of less value.
3. That there was more demand for land in Ulster, either because it was better land or less highly rented.
4. That some form of pressure was operating on the tenants to prevent them purchasing.

* During 1886-87 these figures were more than maintained. In these years 888 sales took place; 389 at ten years' purchase and under, 348 at under twenty years', 108 at under thirty years', and 43 at over thirty years' purchase.

I.—The first of these reasons may give in some slight degree the reason. Owing to the existence of the Ulster custom (*see* p. 74), tenants practically enjoyed the right of Free Sale prior to 1881, and were consequently thoroughly accustomed to avail themselves of its benefits. On the other hand, the peasantry of the rest of Ireland are by no means slow to learn of any alteration in the law which tends to their benefit, and it is quite clear that this reason alone would not suffice to account for the disparity between Ulster and the other provinces.

II.—It is probably true that the best improvements are those in Ulster, but that would be a reason for a smaller number of years' purchase in the other provinces, not for a smaller number of sales.

III.—The third theory is absolutely unwarranted by facts. The land in Ulster is naturally inferior to that in Leinster and Munster, but it is on the average not less highly rented.

IV.—Pressure is, unfortunately, continually put on Southern and Western tenants not to join in the operation of the Free Sale clauses of the Act of 1881. If a tenant is evicted in those districts in which the National League has power, *no matter for what amount of rent, or whether it is justly due or not*, the League refuses invariably to allow bidding at sales. By law, the tenant may sell his good-will in the open market; but if he is evicted, nobody will buy, inasmuch as it is a well-known and indisputable rule of the League that no man may take a farm from which another is evicted. Such a man is called a "land-grabber." Hence the League deprives hundreds of tenants of *what is equivalent to hard cash*, and of what was conferred on them by Mr. Gladstone and the united Liberal Party in 1881.

It is also interesting to observe that in many cases far more is given in Ireland for the tenant's interest than would suffice to buy the fee-simple from the landlord. No landlord in Ireland would dream of getting thirty years' purchase for the fee-simple, yet the preceding table shows that in fifty-eight cases that was given by incoming tenants for the outgoing tenant's interest.

The following cases on the Fishmongers' Estate will illustrate this fact:—

Name of purchasing tenant.	Price paid for tenant's interest under Free Sale.	Price paid for fee-simple to landlord.	Rent.
Boyd	£820 = 41 years' purchase of rent.	£285 = 14½ years' purchase of rent.	£20 0 0
Coyle	£800 = 19 ,,	£594 = 14½ ,,	£40 16 0
Craig	£800 = 21 ,,	£539 = 14½ ,,	£37 0 0
Hamilton	£275 = 42 ,,	£95 = 14½ ,,	£6 10 0
Shannon	£620 = 27 ,,	£331 = 14½ ,,	£22 10 0

THE ARREARS ACT, 1882.

It is generally stated that the "Arrears" question has never been dealt with in Ireland, and that the failure to settle it on the part of the Imperial Parliament is a proof of the incompetence of that body to settle the Irish Land Question.

How untrue is the statement can only be realised by those who know that in 1882 an Arrears Act was passed for Ireland.

That Act provided that those tenants whose valuation for rating purposes was below £30 per annum—that is, the tenants of 88·6 of the holdings (*see* p. 55)—should be given a fresh start. They were enabled, no matter how many years' rent they owed, to clear themselves by the payment of *one year's rent.* The Government paid the landlord another year's rent out of the fund of the Disestablished Church, and wiped out by Act of Parliament the residue of the tenant's debt. Of course the Court had, in justice both to the landlord and the country, to inquire as to the ability or inability of the tenant to pay.

Under this Act 126,882 holdings were benefited. The

annual rental of these holdings was £1,185,265, and £1,820,586 of arrears was absolutely wiped out. (*See* Parliamentary Return presented in 1884 by the Land Commission, of which the following is a summary):—

	Holdings.		Arrears wiped out.
Ulster	41,134		£561,391
Munster	18,994		341,198
Leinster	12,879		223,902
Connaught	52,883		634,333
Extra cases under Sect. 16 of Act ...	992	...	59,762
Total ...	126,882		£1,820,586

THE LAND PURCHASE ACT, 1885 AND 1888.

THIS Act, commonly known as Lord Ashbourne's Act, conferred on Irish tenants opportunities of purchasing their holdings of an altogether exceptional kind, by providing that—

If a tenant wishes to buy his holding, and arranges with his landlord as to terms, he can change his position from that of a perpetual rent-payer into that of the payer of an annuity terminable at the end of 49 years, and less in amount than the annual rent.

Thus, suppose the landlord agrees to take 20 years' purchase or twenty rents for the fee-simple of his land—and Irish landlords, as a rule, are willing to take this sum *or less*—the Government supply the tenant with the necessary purchase money, and he repays the Government at the rate of 4 per cent. per annum, which covers both principal and interest.

The annuities payable on November 1st, 1886, have been paid—*every penny*. Those due on May 1st, 1887, have all been paid but 69—less than 1 per cent. Of those payable on November 1st, 1887, 98½ per cent. have already been paid.

The following table will illustrate the difference between the rent—which, of course, is in most cases a "fair rent" fixed by the Land Court—and the annuity arising out of the 4 per cent. payable to the Government, according to the number of years' purchase which the tenant agrees to pay :—

Number of years' purchase.			Old rent.		Annuity.		Reduction per cent.
15	...	...	£50	...	£30	...	40
16	...	...	50	...	32	...	36
17	...	...	50	...	34	...	32
18	...	...	50	...	36	...	28
19	...	...	50	...	38	...	24
20	...	...	50	...	40	...	20

At the end of 49 years the tenant who so purchases will own the land altogether. If he dies, his children will so own it ; but he is not without benefits in the interim. In the first place, his rent is largely abated ; in the second place, his share in the ownership of his holding is becoming larger every day, and the farm is increasing in market value should he wish to dispose of his interest under the Free Sale provisions of the Act of 1881.

The following cases will suffice as recent examples of benefits accruing to the tenants (1888) from the Land Purchase Act of 1885 :—

Lord Shannon's Estate.—The tenants have purchased at a little over twelve years' purchase of the rents. That means that for every £100 of rent they had to pay year after year, they have now to pay £50 for forty-nine years to the Government.

Lord Lansdowne's Estate.—On the property of Borrowhouse, Queen's County, the tenantry have agreed to purchase at eighteen years' purchase, all arrears to be forgiven on payment of half a year's rent. Leaving the arrears question aside, that means that for every £100 of rent from year to year, they have undertaken to pay the Government £72 for forty-nine years.

Up to date, advances have been made to purchase 3,891 holdings rented under £10, 3,234 holdings rented between £10 and £30, and 884 holdings rented over £30. The entire £5,000,000 allocated for the purpose has been applied. The following table is of interest :—

Loans applied for to April 30th, 1888.			Loans sanctioned to April 30th, 1888.		
Province.	No.	Amount.	Province.	No.	Amount.
Ulster	7,151	£2,035,149	Ulster	5,813	£1,640,120
Leinster	2,025	1,276,097	Munster	1,535	970,104
Munster	2,233	1,564,932	Leinster	1,746	1,219,518
Connaught	1,388	365,485	Connaught	918	243,407
Total	12,797	£5,242,663	Total	10,012	£4,073,149

Parnellite Misrepresentations of the Purchase Act.

The following absurd comments on the Land Purchase Act are from the pen of Mr. J. J. Clancy, M.P. They are in keeping with the Parnellite obstruction to every useful piece of legislation concerning Ireland, and are only noticed here because that member of Mr. Parnell's party has put them into print to depreciate the Land Laws and the Imperial Parliament. He says :—

(*a*) "The tenant may wish to buy, but the landlord need not sell if he likes.

(*b*) The landlord may demand what price he likes—such a price that it would swamp the tenants utterly to pay it.

(*c*) The whole of the purchase-money is not really advanced by the State, for the fifth of it must be left as security with the Land Court.

(*d*) The Government have at present little more than a million of money to help the 500,000 tenants of Ireland to buy their holdings, and consequently could accommodate with advances only the smallest fraction of the entire number.

(*e*) The Government need not and do not always lend the money, even when an agreement has been come to between the landlord and the tenant. In fact, they have often refused to advance any money, because of the wretched quality of the land, or because they did not consider it a sufficient security."

The following considerations show the absolute dishonesty of the line of argument pursued :—

(*a*) The landlord could not be compelled to sell, or the tenant to buy, unless the State fixed a price, which would please nobody.

(*b*) This statement is quite absurd. Technically, of course, it is possible, but what landlord in Ireland would refuse to sell at the fair market value? It might be said with equal truth that "the tenants can offer what price they like." Of course, the landlord can ask a high price, but the tenant is not harmed by that if he refuses to give it; while if he assents to too high a price the Land Commission must protect him. (See *e.*)

(*c*) Four-fifths of the purchase-money is paid over to the landlord at once. The other fifth is retained by the Government, who, however, pay 3 per cent. for it to the depositor. This fifth of the purchase-money is called the "guarantee deposit." The tenant may supply it if he can, in which case he gets 3 per cent. per annum for it, while the landlord is paid off altogether. The landlord, however, is frequently willing to let one-fifth of the purchase-money stand out, in which case he gets 3 per cent. on it, and the tenant need not spend a farthing. At the end of eighteen years the guarantee deposit is paid over to whoever is entitled to it. If to the tenant, it is an enormous boon, for by spending it on redeeming some years of his annuity, he can reduce the period from about forty-nine years to thirty-six. As a matter of practice and fact, the provision about the guarantee deposit is an extra boon to the tenant who has saved some money, and it has proved *no obstacle whatever* to any tenant without money, as landlords are everywhere willing to take four-fifths of the purchase-money and 3 per cent. on the remaining fifth.

(*d*) It will hardly be credited that this statement comes from a member of a party which, for selfish ends and to keep Ireland in discontent, has determinedly opposed any further grant. It should be remembered, (1) that £5,000,000 was allocated for Land Purchase under the Act of 1885; (2) that the sum was found to be sufficient for the time, and has now been exhausted; (3) that of the annuities payable by tenants 95 per cent. and more has been repaid; (4) that a further sum of £5,000,000 has now been applied to the purpose; and (5) last, and most important of all, that in the present downward grade of matters agricultural, thousands of men are naturally unwilling to purchase land.

(*e*) Of the last complaint it can only be said that the Government will lend the money *willingly* if the landlord is robbed, and charges too little. If, however, the landlord charges too much, they will protect the tenant. The "wretched quality" of the land means in this case nothing, save in so far as it affects price. If a landlord asks too much for "wretched" land, the Land Commission will not sanction the sale, because the security for repayment is obviously insufficient.

It is to be hoped that these considerations will serve to dispel several bushels of Parnellite dust.*

* An outrageous attempt has been made to represent large landlords as walking off with so much plunder, as if the money they had got was not *in exchange for land surrendered by them.* They have "walked off" *without the land.*

THE LAND LAW AMENDMENT ACT OF 1887.

THE privileges conferred on Irish tenants by this Act are as follow:—

1. It permits all leaseholders whose leases would expire within 99 years after the passing of the Act to go into Court if they wish, and GET THEIR CONTRACTS BROKEN, and a JUDICIAL RENT FIXED. (Secs. 1, 2.)

   Thus 100,000 non-perpetuity leaseholders, whose claims Mr. Gladstone always insisted on refusing to recognise, have been given the privilege of getting their rents adjusted in accordance with the fall in prices under the Act of 1881.

2. In view of the fall in agricultural produce the Land Commission is empowered and directed to VARY THE RENTS fixed by the Land Courts during the years 1881, 1882, 1883, 1884, and 1885, *in accordance with the difference in prices* between those years and 1887, 1888, and 1889. (Sect. 29.)

   In other words, it was alleged, and alleged with truth, that some "fair rents" fixed between 1881–85 had since become too high, in consequence of the continued fall in prices. Accordingly provision was made for this.

   The Commissioners published during Christmas week, 1887, the result of their revision, and reduced rents from 6 to 20 per cent., according to the varying conditions of different districts. The average was 14 per cent., or about £360,000 per annum.

   A further revision was made during Christmas week, 1888. Prices being admittedly higher than in 1887, the abatement granted has not been quite so large, whereupon the Parnellites declare that the "rents have been raised!" This is in hope that ignorant people may believe that the Unionist Government has raised the old contract rents lowered by the Land Commission.

3. In the case of tenants whose valuation for rating purposes does not exceed £50 (that is, *in the case of 94 per cent. of all tenants—the poorer 94 per cent.*) the Court before which proceedings are taken for the recovery of *any* debt due by the tenant is empowered to stay his eviction, and may give him liberty to pay by instalments, and can extend the time for such payment as it thinks proper. (Sect. 30.)

In accordance with this section evictions were stayed between August 23rd, 1887, and November 23rd, 1888, in **3,254** cases, and "extension" orders (to pay by instalments) were granted as follow:—

2,794	tenants	were	allowed	1	year.
227	"	"	"	2	years.
79	"	"	"	3	"
31	"	"	"	4	"
223	"	"	"	5	"

(*See* Parliamentary Returns.)

4. If a tenant applies to the Land Commission Court to have a "fair rent" fixed, his "fair rent" dates, not from the decision of the Court, but from the time of his application; and if in the interval he has paid more than the "fair rent" the landlord has to refund it.

The Real Argument from the Land Acts.

It must be remembered that the Unionist Party do not contend that the land laws of Ireland are perfect. Their contention is threefold, and is as follows:—

1. That the Irish people have now no pre-eminent land grievances, but are in an incomparably better position

than the tenantry of any other country in the civilised world; and

2. That the measures already passed prove the willingness and competence of the Imperial Parliament to legislate for Ireland.

3. That the Unionist Party is willing to do all that is just witness the Act of 1887.

IRISH TENANTS *VERSUS* ENGLISH OR SCOTCH TENANTS.

1. The Irish tenant has, but the British tenant has not, compensation for all permanent improvements. It will be said that Irish tenants are entitled to this as having made them, and British tenants are not. This is, *as a rule*, true; but the fact that Irish tenants have the compensation destroys any grievance.

2. The Irish tenant has fixity of tenure: the British tenant has not.

3. The Irish tenant has a Court to fix his rent for him: the British tenant has to pay the full market value.

4. The Irish tenant can sell the good-will of his farm before or after eviction: the British tenant cannot do so.

5. The Irish tenant can buy his holding by paying less for it for forty-nine years than the annual rent: the British tenant cannot.

6. In 1882 the tenantry occupying 88 per cent. of the holdings of Ireland got the chance of getting arrears of rent obliterated. No like chance has ever been given to English or Welsh tenantry, and only to farmers in seven out of twenty-six Scotch counties.

7. Irish leaseholders can break their leases: British leaseholders cannot do so.

8. The Irish tenant can have his rent varied by Act of Parliament in proportion to the market prices.

These are some important distinctions thus tabulated.

ATTITUDE OF THE PARNELLITES TOWARDS THE LAND ACTS.

Sometimes, for political purposes, the Parnellites adopt a different line of action towards the Land Acts. They occasionally claim credit for having got them passed. The actual facts may be noted.

The 1870 Act, giving compensation for improvements, was passed long before the Parnellites were ever heard of. If credit is due to any Irish member, it is entirely to the Ulster Liberals, who contended for this measure for years; and therefore Mr. T. W. Russell and Mr. Lea have far more right to claim credit for this measure as passed by *their* predecessors than have any Parnellites.

In 1881 the Parnellites declined to vote for the great measure which conferred the "three F's" on the Irish tenantry. They walked out of the House.

In the same year Mr. Gladstone put Mr. Parnell in gaol, on the following charge (*see* Parliamentary Returns, February 1, 1882):—

"Inciting other persons wrongfully, and without legal authority, to intimidate divers persons with a view to compel them to abstain from doing what they had a legal right to do—namely, to apply to the Court, under the provisions of the Land Law (Ireland) Act, 1881, to have a fair rent fixed for their holdings."

On September 17, 1881, Mr. Parnell had sent the following telegram:—

"To Collins, President Land League, Boston. The Convention has just closed after three days' session. Resolutions were adopted for National Self-government, the unconditional liberation of the land for the people, tenants *not to use the rent-fixing clauses of the Land Act*, and follow old Land League lines, and rely upon old methods to secure justice. The Executive of the League is empowered to select test-cases, in order that tenants in surrounding districts may realise, by the result of cases decided, the hollowness of the Act."

As regards the Act of 1885, they have always tried to dissuade tenants from purchasing their holdings. This has been done on general grounds, and not on account of any particular terms offered, while they vigorously opposed its extension in 1888.

The Act of 1887 was described in the House of Commons by Mr. Parnell as "a stab in the back."

A complete settlement by the House of Commons of the Arrears question was prevented chiefly by the exertions of Mr. John Dillon, M.P. (*Vide* p. 105.)

It may also be of interest to note the extraordinary change which Gladstonians generally have adopted towards these Acts. Once they were splendid measures, which had redressed all the land grievances of Ireland; now they are evidently of no account, and the great Liberal measures of the past were so many fiascos which did no useful service whatever.

It may be further serviceable to remind Gladstonians who claim, as is sometimes done, the whole credit of the measures of 1870 and 1881 for their Party, that these measures were passed by a united Liberal Party, and that of the survivors of the Cabinets of 1870 and 1881, which passed these Acts, the large majority of the members are Liberal Unionists.

The Present Position of the Irish Landlord.

So much nonsense is talked about the grievances of Irish tenants that it may be sometimes useful to consider the matter from the standpoint of an Irish landlord. This may serve to clear the air. The following points are suggested :—

1. An Irish landlord has land. He finds tenants on it who have been there under his predecessors. What can he do?

2. He cannot charge an excessive rent—how can he The tenant can get a "fair rent" fixed, which he cannot add a penny to. But if the tenant has not or cannot get a "fair rent" fixed, how can the landlord even then charge an excessive rent? He can only charge the market value. Besides, the tenant can stay eviction by applying to have a "fair rent" fixed.

3. It is absurd to pretend that the landlord—unless he is an utter fool—can attempt to charge more than the tenant can pay. If he does, he will not get it; and if he evicts, what will happen then?

4. In considering this, we put out of sight any difficulties the landlord may encounter in consequence of resistance. The more resistance, the more costly to the landlord. If the landlord evicts peacefully, what is his position?

5. He can plainly only evict if the eviction is for non-payment of a just rent. Otherwise he is a loser, for no one will take the farm, so he is himself punished. If, however, another tenant can be got to make and pay the rent, it must be a fair rent. If so, why should not the landlord have it?

6. However, the landlord proceeds to evict. The old method of procedure by distraint is practically and actually obsolete. The landlord can only proceed by eviction if one year's rent is due. He serves notice on the defaulting tenant. Forthwith the tenant can serve notice of compensation for improvements. If the landlord has made the improvements, and can prove that he has made them, of course the tenant will not get, and ought not to get, compensation; if, however, the tenant has made them, *or if this is doubtful*, the tenant must be compensated before he

can be evicted. Of course, if the tenant owes more rent than the value of the improvements, he will not get compensation from his landlord: but why should he?

7. However, if the tenant be a poorer tenant (that is, under £15 valuation), as are 70 per cent. of the tenants, he can also make the landlord give him compensation for disturbance if the rent is unfair.

8. So far it is quite obvious that the landlord is dissuaded alike by law and his own interest from unjust eviction.

9. If, however, the tenant likes, he can sell the good-will of the farm. Of course the debt must be paid to the landlord out of the sum. Again, why should it not be so paid? But the League may, and does, forbid bidders at a sale, and the tenant's interest may indeed be knocked down to the landlord for little or nothing. But what can he then do? The interest is no use to him. Why should he not have it cheap if it has no market value, and what can he do with it if the rent is unfair? No one will buy it to get the farm at an impossible rent.

10. But the landlord may proceed for rent, not by eviction, but as a debt. If the amount is over £100 he can proceed in the Superior Courts by writ of summons; and plaint, if under £100, in the Courts of Quarter Session. If the position is thoroughly just, why should he not have this benefit? If, however, it is unjust, how does he gain? He will secure no tenant, his land will be derelict, and he will be the loser.

11. Finally, whether the landlord proceeds by writ of ejectment, or an ordinary writ of *fieri facias*, he will find that, under Section 30 of the Act of 1887, if the debtor can show that his inability to pay did not

arise from his own conduct, act, and default, the Court will stay execution, and make an order for deferred payment by instalments—certainly no boon to the landlord.

These points are recommended as an antidote to the pernicious nonsense talked daily by people who are either ignorant of, or anxious to conceal, the real facts. (*See* Arrears, p. 91; and Evictions, p. 106.)

Many, though not all, of the rights of the Irish tenant have now been explained. It is now necessary to deal plainly with the subject from another standpoint, and to investigate two matters with reference to which the Unionist Party generally, and the Liberal Unionists in particular, have been attacked. These two points are, (1) non-treatment of the arrears question, and (2) the rejection of a Bill introduced by Mr. Parnell in 1886.

ARREARS.

In connection with this question the following points are of prime importance :—

(*a*) The Arrears Act of 1882. (*See* p. 91.)

(*b*) The fallacy of representing arrears of unrevised rents as exorbitant. Rents have been reduced because they had become too high owing to a fall in prices. It by no means follows that a rent of £36, reduced to £25 in 1887, should have been £25 in 1878 or 1881.

(*c*) As before stated, arrears are no obstacle to getting a fair rent fixed. It has been said that a landlord can threaten a tenant with eviction for arrears to deter him from applying to have a fair rent fixed. That would do the landlord no good whatever, and it is doubtful if a single case could be pointed out in which what is suggested occurred. Legal possibilities are not actual facts.

(*d*) Government has already offered to deal with any outstanding question of arrears on certain lines well within the memory of the public. An offer was made in 1887 to give any insolvent tenant a fresh start on a declaration of his full indebtedness to all his creditors and the payment of as much in the pound as the Court should deem reasonable. This suggestion, put forth in the House of Commons by Mr. Chamberlain, was accepted by the Government, *assented to by Sir William Harcourt and the Gladstonian Opposition*, but contemptuously rejected by the Nationalist representatives.

(*e*) Irish landlords have not been asking their tenants for old arrears calculated at anything like their full amount. (*See* Plan of Campaign, p. 117.)

It can hardly be necessary to point out that the reason given by the Parnellites for rejecting the proposed settlement of the arrears question was that it would prevent the shopkeepers of Ireland from realising what was due to them. They objected to the tenant who was in debt arranging with *all his creditors*. But why not? It was postulated without a show of reason, but with plenty of high-flown rhetoric, that the landlord's debt was unjust, but the shopkeeper's just. Certainly it is well to remember the famous dictum of Sir William Harcourt —"The landowner has just as good a right to a fair rent as you or I have to the coat upon our back." * (Speech at Glasgow, October 25th, 1881.)

THE REJECTION OF MR. PARNELL'S BILL OF 1886.

No one can attach the faintest blame to the Unionist Party for rejecting this Bill who cares to know what its provisions were.

In it Mr. Parnell asked for relief for about 100,000 yearly tenants. These 100,000 were those who had had fair rents fixed before December 31st, 1884.

* Liberals are invited to compare this sentiment with that of Mr. T. P. O'Connor, M.P., and of Father Sheehy on page 129.

He asked for relief for them on the ground that prices had fallen to a considerable degree in 1886, and that the rents fixed before December 31st, 1884, had become too high: while he deliberately abstained from asking for any relief for tenants who had not got fair rents fixed.

What were the facts? Up to August, 1882, the Land Commissioners after full investigation, and with full knowledge of facts and prices, had reduced rents 20·5 per cent.; up to August, 1883, 19·5 per cent.; in the next year (1884) 18·7 per cent.; in 1885, 18·1 per cent.; and in 1886 they made reductions of 24·1 per cent.

In other words, the judges, whose business it was to know, were reporting at the time to the country that, owing to the further fall in prices, about 5½ per cent., at the most, should be knocked off the 1882, 1883, and 1884 rents.

This modest idea did not suit Mr. Parnell; he proposed to pay the landlord in these cases only 50 per cent. of the fair rent, and to send the remainder into Courts for which he provided no machinery!

He further proposed, for no reason at all, to stop arrears of these same fair rents to the extent of 50 per cent.!

He further provided that in case the landlord had taken steps to recover his debt he should get nothing at all; but, to punish him, 50 per cent. should be paid *into Court*, not to the landlord, pending a decision about the other half.

There was one provision in the Bill which would have had a good chance of immediate adoption only for the clauses just mentioned—that opening the Land Courts to leaseholders. This was done, however, in the next Session of Parliament.

[For the alleged connection between the Plan of Campaign and the rejection of this Bill, *see* p. 127.]

EVICTIONS.

THE entire subject of evictions can be best divided into three parts, dealing with the Law of Eviction, the Facts and Figures of Evictions, and the Causes of Eviction.

THE LAW OF EVICTION.

The following are the most important points :—

1. No tenant can be evicted in consequence of a writ of ejectment for non-payment of rent unless he owes a year's rent.

2. He may, however, be ejected *on title* if sued for a debt due, and if judgment is given against him. In this case his goods and interest may be put up for auction by the sheriff. How seldom this method is resorted to, figures will prove. The landlord has, however, no more to say to this than has the shopkeeper, or the publican, or the "gombeen man"—*i.e.*, the local money-lender.

3. If evicted for non-payment of rent, the process is as follows :—The landlord obtains his judgment,* and then a period of six weeks must elapse before he can proceed further. During these six weeks the tenant can stay eviction by payment in full, or settlement.

4. Prior to the passing of the Land Act of 1887 the landlord next proceeded, in case of a failure to settle, to evict the tenant. The tenant then evicted had a period of six months, during which time he might redeem. He was no longer a tenant, but by paying what was due, or coming to a settlement with his landlord, he could be reinstated, *as he was in the vast majority of cases.* Of course, the land was for these six months absolutely useless to the landlord.

5. During the six months while the tenant was out of possession, the landlord was liable to him for the crops on the land, and for the profits he (the landlord) *might* have made.

* This judgment, or "ejectment decree," is sometimes confounded with "eviction notices" and with physical evictions.

6. As a result of this last provision, it happened that after eviction the landlord (in how many cases, figures will tell) reinstated the tenant as a caretaker, though not with the rights of a tenant. At the end of the six months the period of redemption expired. The tenant was on the land as caretaker. If he settled, he became a tenant; if not, and if he refused possession, a second physical removal might have to take place. Having lost his tenancy, he became a trespasser.

7. Of course, in addition to what is stated above, it must never be forgotten that the tenant could secure the value of improvements made by him, by compensation or by the benefit of Free Sale. These matters have already been described at length under the Acts of 1870 and 1881.

8. An important change was made in the law by the Act of 1887. This Act placed the physical eviction at the end of the six months allowed for redemption, instead of at the beginning. It provided that in all cases where the rent was under £100 (that is, in over 94 per cent. of the holdings of Ireland) the landlord who was entitled to evict should not resort to physical eviction in the first instance. A written notice sent to the tenant, after judgment had been obtained, and at the termination of a series of legal proceedings of which he must be fully cognisant, makes him a caretaker. He then has six months to redeem, and does redeem in the vast majority of instances.

9. These written notices are known as "eviction" notices, but they precede actual eviction by six months. In the overwhelming majority of cases actual eviction never succeeds. The most laughable mistakes have been made on this subject, as by Lord Ripon, who, speaking in October, 1888, spoke of many thousand

evictions as likely to take place in Ireland because of the number of eviction notices; while some thousand eviction notices in the preceding quarter had been followed by only eighty-six evictions!* Sir George Trevelyan, speaking at Hexham on the 28th of September, 1889, without Lord Ripon's excuse of ignorance, stated that "in 1888, 9,752 families lost their homes in Ireland." The statement, which certainly conveyed to his hearers the idea that these persons were left desolate and homeless by eviction, was in that sense *absolutely untrue.*

THE FACTS AND FIGURES OF EVICTIONS.

Are there really many evictions in Ireland? Do the landlords there evict as is alleged, wholesale? Any one would think so whose reading was confined to the Gladstonian and Nationalist press.

On this subject every method of exaggeration is employed. There are, however, seven distinct methods employed in this connection to trap the unwary. These are:—

1. The use of extravagant language.
2. The confusion of persons with families, by the artful employment of which trick the Parnellites make evictions appear about seven times as numerous as they really are.
3. The assumption that of the total number of evictions all are by landlords.
4. The absolute ignoring of the fact that many evicted tenants are at once reinstated as tenants.
5. The absolute ignoring of the fact that very many evicted tenants are readmitted as caretakers, and ultimately redeem their position as tenants.

* In 1888 only 773 evictions took place, but there are about 550,000 tenant farmers in Ireland.

6. The confusion of eviction notices (*see* p. 108) with evictions.
7. The assumption that if the landlord anywhere evicts a tenant, the landlord alone is to blame.

As to the first of these, *the use of extravagant language*, we shall give one specimen of Parnellite methods. Speaking in the House of Commons in August. 1886, Mr. Parnell said: "If it were not for 'moonlighting,' Lord Kenmare would not leave a roof over the heads of any of his tenants"—while *United Ireland* described the same landlord as the "Evictor-General of Ireland." What are the facts? Lord Kenmare holds 91,000 acres, on which are 1,800 tenants. In the seven years 1860-66 he evicted nine tenants, or $1\frac{2}{7}$ per annum. Such was the conduct of the "Evictor-General," and such is the invariable method of the Parnellite press.

A favourite Parnellite trick is to *confuse persons with families*. At election times a Parnellite placard is generally exhibited, stating that during the last fifty years 3,668,000 Irish persons have been evicted! The authority given for this statement is a work called "Fifty Years' National Progress," by Michael G. Mulhall.

The following is Mr. Mulhall's statement in his own words:—

"Official returns give the number of families, and these averaging seven persons, we ascertain the actual number of persons evicted:—

	Years.	Families.	Persons.
False.	1849-51	263,000	1,841,000
	1852-60	110,000	770,000
	1861-70	47,000	329,000
	1871-86	104,000	728,000
	Total	524,000	3,668,000."

The foregoing is Mr. Mulhall's statement, given on pp. 114 and 115 of his book. What are the facts?

The official returns give, not what Mr. Mulhall alleges, but the following figures:—

	Years.		Families.		Persons.
True.	1849–51		49,000	...	263,000
	1852–60		22,000	...	110,000
	1861–70		9,700	...	47,000
	1871–86	... ...	20,000	...	104,000
		Total	100,700		524,000

In other words, PERSONS in the official returns were transmuted into FAMILIES, then the figures were multiplied by 7 to make them persons, and so the current Parnellite numbers are based on a calculation which makes every Irish farmer the parent of about 35 children.

As a matter of actual fact, about 100,000 families, and 524,000 persons, are given in the official returns as evicted between 1849 and 1886. That means 100,000 evictions in 38 years, which on an average is less than 3,000 evictions a year. Whether this number is large or small can only be determined after patient investigation. The following considerations help to determine it:—

The official returns as quoted include every case where the eviction was followed by readmission, either as tenant or caretaker, and also every case whether eviction was at the suit of the landlord or not; also every eviction in the towns of Ireland, Dublin alone excepted.

In 1887 a vigorous attempt was made by the Irish Loyal and Patriotic Union to investigate every case of eviction in Ireland which had taken place during the year 1886. In that year there were **3,781** evictions, representing **19,500** persons. The figures appeared very large to unthinking persons, but investigation soon reduced them to their proper proportions.

Full particulars were obtained in **3,024** of these evictions, with the following results:—

434, or **14** per cent., were out of dwelling-houses in cities and towns, and so quite unconnected with the land question.

67, or 2 per cent., were out of accommodation holdings held by persons living in a town. These holdings are not agricultural, and were, therefore, rigidly excluded by Mr. Gladstone from the Act of 1881.

305, or over 10 per cent., were cases where no physical eviction could take place because no one resided on the holdings. The tenant had either lived on an adjacent farm or had left the place derelict.

198 cases, or over 6 per cent., were "on title." On investigation it turned out that these were either cases of (1) trespassers unlawfully squatting on land to which they had not any right, (2) persons wrongfully in possession under disputed wills, or (3) cases where the local shopkeeper or money-lender bought up and sold the interest of the tenant to pay his debt.

The cases already enumerated reduce the 3,024 cases of eviction to 2,020. In other words, 33 per cent.—one-third—disappear at once.

The further reductions are, however, still more remarkable. In 518 cases, about 17 per cent. of the total, the tenants were reinstated *as tenants.* In other words, they were able to pay, and did pay; or, if not, they were leniently treated.

In 916 cases, however, the tenants were readmitted as caretakers, pending redemption—that is, in almost one-third of the entire number. Now these 916 either came to a settlement with their landlord in the six months, or they did not. Whether they did or not, they were not by eviction deprived, as Englishmen and Scotchmen often think, of their interest. They had six months in which they might sell their interest, as already explained, for a sum far exceeding the landlord's demand, and so depart with the money in their pockets; and this was actually done *in a large number of cases.*

As a matter of fact, however, out of 3,024 evictions only 2,020 were from agricultural holdings with residences attached thereto, and for non-payment of rent. Out of these 2,020 only 586 were cases where the tenants were not immediately readmitted in some form. Of these 586 every evicted tenant was entitled to compensation for improvements, or to the right of Free Sale, and to any profit the landlord might make out of the farm while the tenant was out of possession during the ensuing six months.

There was nothing exceptional about 1886, and there can be no doubt that if other years had been examined in the same way, it would appear that out of 100 recorded evictions, 33 per cent. are unconnected with agriculture, or non-residential, while in at least 45 per cent. tenants are at once readmitted.

We have now seen how 3,024 investigated evictions in Ireland give us really 586. The official number for 1886 was, however, 3,781. Making a liberal allowance we can assume not more than 800 physical evictions as actually taking place in that year. It may be interesting to inquire what proportion these evictions bear to the total number of holdings in the country.

The number of holdings was in that year 560,000, so 800 evictions mean that out of every 700 tenants in Ireland one was evicted, and one only! These figures certainly fail to bear out the extravagant language of the Parnellites.

It is, of course, currently assumed that all evictions arise out of the fault of the landlord. How far this is true will be considered when we come to deal with the Plan of Campaign, under which most recent Irish evictions have taken place. (*See* pp. 117—127.) But it is interesting to know that in all Ireland 862 persons were evicted in 1888, many of whom were subsequently readmitted, while in London and suburbs with an equal population, 1,412 persons were evicted in the same period, not ten of whom were readmitted. Perhaps the following comparison may prove useful :—

EVICTIONS IN AMERICA FOR NON-PAYMENT OF RENT.

Simpson's American statute law gives the following results of the legislation of the States as to evictions :—

"Generally, in all cases of neglect or refusal by any tenant to pay rent, his estate may be determined by the landlord, and he may re-enter"—

On fourteen days' notice in Massachusetts, Michigan, Wisconsin, Minnesota, and Oregon.
On ten days' notice in Indiana, Kansas, and Washington Territory.
Immediately after demand for possession in Illinois, North Carolina, Missouri, and South Carolina.
On seven days' notice in New Hampshire.
On thirty days' notice in Maine.
On fifteen days' notice in Rhode Island.
On three days' notice in Nevada, Colorado, and Louisiana.
On five days' notice in Vermont.

Yet in Ireland, where we are told evictions take place with barbarous celerity, the effect of the law, passed by a "Coercion" Government, is to make six months' notice necessary, even when rent is a whole year in arrear.

Evictions in the Abstract.

It may sometimes be necessary for a speaker distinctly to address an audience on evictions in the abstract, and to ask them distinctly, Are ALL evictions wrong?

It must be carefully remembered that this is a current belief of the Parnellites. They denounce *all* evictions alike, whether these spring from the rapacity of a landlord or the dishonesty of a tenant. Eviction is repeatedly called a *crime*, and no limitation whatever is introduced in the language of the speaker to show that he is referring to the particular circumstances of the case. If this be not so, it would be interesting to learn from a Parnellite of a single eviction which has ever taken place in Ireland of which he or his party have approved. There is not a single case on record where the Parnellites have said to a tenant, "Really, this is reasonable; you ought to pay." *No such case has ever occurred*, for the Parnellite policy is to denounce all evictions alike.

Now, if all evictions are unjust, they ought to be put a stop to at once in Ireland, and in Scotland and England also. The working classes ought, however, to be asked, How would this affect them?

In the first place, the building societies of the country would be bankrupt in three months. They would have lost their right of enforcing payment from a defaulting member.

The price of houses would go up enormously. No one would sell a house he owned save for full cash down. No one would let a house save at a rent sufficiently large to recompense him for the risk of meeting a dishonest tenant.

As for new buildings, that would simply be out of the question. In other words, the abolition of eviction altogether would mean simple ruin to the working classes of the country.*

A clear statement of these facts will at once enable audiences to perceive that before one declaims against eviction, it is necessary to examine the facts of each eviction, and to ascertain whether Irish evictions are just or unjust.

Are Irish Evictions Unjust?

It has already been pointed out at length that eviction does not make a tenant lose his improvements in his holding, or the right to sell his interest; it simply prevents him retaining the landlord's property without paying for it.

The following facts will probably prove of interest:—

In 1886, an average year, the following was the average amount of rent due by Irish tenants who were evicted from agricultural holdings on which they resided:—

Number per cent. of Evicted Tenants.				Amount of Rent due.
11·9		owed		1 year's rent.
17·1	...	"	...	1½ years' rent.
20·2	...	"	...	2 "
13·9	...	"	...	2½ "
13·6	...	"	...	3 "
6·8	...	"	...	3½ "

* This point is admirably explained in "Think It Out," a lecture by Thomas Hodgkin, D.C.L.

Number per cent. of Evicted Tenants.				Amount of Rent due.	
6·5	...	owed	...	4 years' rent.	
1·8	...	,,	...	4½	,,
1·7	...	,,	...	5	,,
1·1	...	,,	...	5½	,,
2·1	...	,,	...	6	,,
3·3	...	owed more than	...	6	,,

THE GLENBEIGH EVICTIONS.

These evictions were, for a long time, utilised for election purposes by the Parnellites, who drew eloquent pictures of the evictions of poor people, while carefully concealing the facts of the case.

They are still constantly alluded to. Mr. Campbell Bannerman, M.P., is reported to have said at Greenock on November 2nd, 1888, that only for the conduct of his opponents there would have been no Glenbeigh in Ireland. This, he alleged, was caused by the failure of the Unionist Party to deal with the question of arrears.

This is a species of reckless assertion which can only be met by the recital of facts.

At Glenbeigh 70 tenants owed £6,177, a sum representing at least 3½ years' rent. The agent was at first willing to take one year's rent and costs, about £1,800, the total rental being £1,731 per annum. At a later date the agent expressed his willingness to take £865 and costs, about £900 in all, and to wipe out £5,312, *including all arrears.* The arrears question had therefore nothing in the world to do with the Glenbeigh evictions. At first all the tenants accepted this offer and promised to pay. As a fact, only 17 paid, but 53 refused to pay anything on gale-day. Their priest wrote of these 53 that they were "poor slaves who would not keep their word." It will scarcely be credited that after the offer of the agent to accept £865, and to forgive £5,312 out of £6,177, and before evictions took place, a document was signed by the following members of Parliament—Messrs. Dillon, Mahony,

E. Harrington, and Conybeare—denouncing the agent's conduct as "barbarous and inhuman."

These are the facts of a stock-case of Parnellite horrors. The usual plan is to try and excite sympathy by pictures of poor persons suffering from eviction, and by the absolute suppression of all facts which would throw light on the justice or injustice of the case.

THE PLAN OF CAMPAIGN.

There can be no dispute as to what the Plan of Campaign is; it was first announced in the supplement to *United Ireland* on Saturday, November 20th, 1886.

Briefly summarised the Plan is as follows:—

The tenantry on a given estate meet, each tenant pledging himself to abide by the decision of the majority, to hold no personal communication with the landlord or his agent, and to accept no terms not given to every one. The rents may be old rents, judicial rents, or fixed in any way. The landlord has probably offered an abatement, possibly an all-round abatement, but not as large as the tenantry want, or he has refused an all-round abatement, but offered separate abatements to each tenant according to circumstances. This offer is refused. The tenants formulate their demand. On gale-day they go to the rent office in a body. If the agent will not see them *all*, they send their chairman, generally the priest, to demand the all-round abatement they require, the well-to-do farmer asking as much as the poor cottier. The landlord is then offered his rent less by this abatement of 30, 40, or 50 per cent. If he takes it, there the matter ends. If he refuses, the money is lodged with trustees—to be used, if necessary, to fight the landlord.

The illegality of the Plan has been distinctly declared by the Courts of Law in the cases of Blunt *v.* Byrne, and of Flowen *v.* Dillon. Its illegality has no connection whatever with the Crimes Act. In England or in Ireland alike any meeting called to advocate it may be dispersed by force, like any other meeting called for any other illegal object.*

The chief apologies put forth for the Plan of Campaign are (1) necessity, (2) that the demands made under it are fair, since the Law Courts have conceded similar abatements, (3) that it never would have originated at all only for the rejection of Mr. Parnell's Bill of 1886.

A short examination of the facts will completely demolish all these defences, and will distinctly prove that the Plan of Campaign has been put in force where these apologies cannot be maintained. It will be advisable to give as instances a brief statement of the leading facts on the chief estates where it has been tried.

The Massereene Estate.

On this estate there are 327 holdings. In 90 the tenants had judicial rents, and had further abatements given them under the Act of 1887. Twenty tenants were leaseholders, and to them, as well as to all the others, the Courts were open. The rental was under the Government valuation. The "arrears" question did not affect this case, for though these were large the landlord offered at once to estimate them as if they had been reduced by the Land Commission. He asked for them on the basis of the latest judicial reductions. In other words, he asked for arrears of "fair" rent, to which he was obviously entitled in common honesty, and not for arrears of a rack-rent. *The Protestant tenants*, 36 *in number, stood out to a man* against the Plan of Campaign. They thought the landlord

* The following are the words of Chief Baron Palles, and it is unnecessary to say that his law has never been impugned:—"Anybody taking part in it [the Plan], aiding it, promoting it, calling a meeting for the purpose of supporting it, was guilty of an offence for which he might be criminally proceeded against. . . . Any meeting for the purpose of promoting the Plan of Campaign was in law an illegal assembly, and the Crown or any magistrate had the power to disperse any meetings called for the purpose."—Feb. 18th, 1888.

fair and reasonable and the "Plan" dishonest. 64 *Roman Catholic tenants also declined to join the conspiracy.* Eight tenants have been evicted, and their farms taken by Protestant tenants from Ulster and Scotland, who are quite willing to pay rent.

The Ponsonby Estate.

This estate is in Cork, and its area is 10,000 acres. The rental is £7,800. The rents have never been raised within the memory of the oldest inhabitant, and so fair are these that out of 300 tenants who might have gone into Court only 50 did so. In 1880 the landlord voluntarily gave abatements of from 15 to 20 per cent., and forgave some thousands of pounds of arrears. In 1886 the landlord voluntarily offered abatements of 20 per cent. on non-judicial and 10 per cent. on judicial rents; he was also willing to forgive all arrears on payment of one year's rent. In other words, he was willing to forego £6.000 of debt. The rents were collected from the tenants by Mr. Lane, M.P., for the Plan; and the landlord got nothing. He was obliged to evict 9 tenants.

Such was the condition of affairs at the close of 1888. Since when Mr. Smith Barry, M.P., and a syndicate formed by him, have purchased the estate from Mr. Ponsonby. Mr. Smith Barry's company then offered the tenants their farms on certain terms of purchase, or that they could remain as tenants under a fair rent fixed by the Land Court; any decision of that Court to be regarded as retrospective, *so as to cover arrears.*

The Kingston Estate.

This estate is close to Mitchelstown, County Cork, and belongs to the Countess of Kingston. There are 700 agricultural tenants, 550 of whom were granted leases by the late earl, for which they publicly thanked him and gave him an illuminated address. Rent was always well paid without complaint, and in 1880 there were practically no arrears. Then came the

"No Rent" manifesto, and the entire case altered. In 1881 the leaseholders were allowed and invited to go into Court and get "fair rents" fixed, but only one of the 550 leaseholders would do so. In 1886 the tenants demanded a uniform abatement of 20 per cent.; the landlord offered from 10 to 25 per cent., to vary according to individual circumstances. This offer was, *on the average*, the same as that of the Campaigners, but very different in fact. Under the Plan the well-to-do farmer was to get as much as the poor cottier; under the landlord's sliding scale large relief was offered to the poor, and little or nothing to those who were able to pay. Accordingly Mr. William O'Brien, M.P., Mr. John O'Connor, M.P., and Dr. Tanner, M.P., collected the rents for the Plan on December 8th, 1886. In December, 1887, the Land Act of that year came into force. Many tenants who had been leaseholders, 545 in all, went into Court. Judgment was speedily delivered in 120 cases, in which the rental of £2,668 was reduced by £511. This, being an average reduction of 20 per cent., was claimed as an indication that the demand of the Plan of Campaign was just, but it actually corroborated the landlord's sliding scale, giving no reduction whatever in some cases, and a large reduction in others.

The Luggacurran Estate.

This estate is in the Queen's County, and belongs to the Marquis of Lansdowne. Almost all the tenants are non-judicial tenants, very few being leaseholders, and very few having asked the Courts to fix their rents. The rental is £7,000, out of which the landlord allows £1,100 to be annually spent on the estate. In 1886 the tenants demanded 35 per cent. on *non-judicial* and 25 per cent on *judicial* rents, threatening to adopt the Plan of Campaign as an alternative. The landlord refused this demand, but offered to give reductions varying from 15 per cent. to 25 per cent. on non-judicial rents. There was no question as to the ability of the tenants to pay, Mr. Denis Kilbride, M.P., stating as follows:—

"The Luggacurran evictions differed from most of the other evictions to this extent—that *they were able to pay the rent;* it was a fight of intelligence against intelligence; it was diamond cut diamond." (*Freeman's Journal*, March 30th, 1887.) The Marquis of Lansdowne was obliged ultimately to enforce his rights, and several tenants were evicted, among them Mr. Kilbride, who occupied a large farm of over 700 acres, with a modern residence and large outhouses (all built by the landlord), at a rental of £760. Another evicted tenant was Mr. John Dunne, renting a large farm of 1,304 acres. This gentleman was able to enter a racehorse for the Curragh after his eviction. *All the Protestants on this estate refused to join the Plan, and all paid their rents.*

The O'Grady Estate.

The rental on this estate was never raised, nor was there ever an eviction on the O'Grady property till after the Plan of Campaign. The rental, which in 1881 amounted to £2,108, was reduced after a report by a valuator in 1882 to £1,616. There were forty-two tenants, and in 1883 thirty-eight of these took leases. In 1885 The O'Grady gave a further abatement of from 15 to 25 per cent., subject to which the rent *was cheerfully paid.* In October, 1886, he gave orders to the agent to give a similar abatement; but Father Ryan, C.C., told the tenants to demand 30 per cent. on judicial and 40 on non-judicial rents. Ultimately the Plan was persisted in, and six tenants were evicted.

It was in connection with this estate that the case of Tom Moroney occurred. Moroney's rent was £85. For that he had a large public-house, five small houses, the tolls of the Herbertstown fairs, and thirty-seven acres of land. The tolls alone amounted in value to between £50 and £60 per annum. The landlord offered an abatement to Moroney of 25 per cent.—that is, he asked for £64, which Moroney was notoriously able to pay. When a writ was issued, Moroney sold his cattle under what is called a Plan of Campaign auction, whereupon the money was lodged with trustees. Moroney was accordingly declared a bankrupt, *as he would have been in England or Scotland.* For refusing to be sworn in court, lest he should have to tell what became of his goods, thus fraudulently hidden away, he was subsequently put in prison, *as he would have been in England or Scotland.* He could have got out of prison any day by abandoning the fraud and answering the Court, *as he also could in England or Scotland.* For months his friends represented that he was dying in gaol, both his mind and body being injuriously affected. Suddenly he was released at the request of the landlord, whereupon his health was immediately alleged by the same parties to have been improved during his stay in prison.

The Brooke, or Coolgreany Estate.

This estate is in the County of Wexford, near Coolgreany. The landlord has made all the improvements in the estate without ever raising the rent. In 1881 an abatement of 25 per cent. was made, and the tenantry were urged to get fair rents fixed. Acting on the advice of the Land League, they refused to avail themselves of the Act of 1881, and demanded other abatements instead. This was refused, and forty writs were issued, whereupon they *all paid full rents* at once. There are 114 tenants—15 have judicial rents, 22 are leaseholders, and 77 are non-judicial tenants. In 1886 the Plan of Campaign was started. The following were the demands of the tenantry:—(1) That an all-round reduction of 30 per cent. should be given; (2) that a Protestant named Webster should be evicted from a farm for which he had paid the rent; and (3) that a Roman Catholic named Lenehan, who had not paid and had been evicted, should be reinstated. Eighty tenants joined the Plan, and Sir Thomas Esmonde, M.P., and Mr. Mayne, M.P., took their money. *All the Protestants on the estate* paid their rents less the abatement offered, were quite satisfied, and *declined to have anything to do with the Plan of Campaign.* Ultimately evictions commenced, and 70 holdings were cleared. Coolgreany has since been "planted." Of course, the tenants who refused to join in "The Plan" have been boycotted, though they had a perfect right to refuse if they chose.

The Vandeleur Estate.

This estate is in the County Clare; it consists of 20,000 acres, and there are 800 tenants. In 1873, after a succession of good seasons, rents were raised, but to a figure much below the average rental of the country or of the County Clare. If the rents so raised were fair, the tenants had no cause for complaint; if they were unfair, they had no cause for complaint either, inasmuch as they were allowed not to pay, so that in 1881 they owed £30,000 of arrears. In the same year the Land Act passed, and in 1882 came the Arrears Act, which wiped out the entire arrears of nearly every tenant. By the end of 1882 the arrears of £30,000 had disappeared. Out of the 800 tenants, 200 only asked for judicial rents, the remaining 600 being satisfied with the landlord's treatment. In September, 1886, the agent made an offer of 20 per cent. reduction on non-judicial rents. *Two hundred and fifty of the tenants received these terms gladly, and paid at once.* Two months later Messrs. Cox, M.P., and Jordan, M.P., visited the estate, and the Plan of Campaign was started. The poorer tenantry were, however, forbidden to join, so only 120 of the wealthier farmers did so; they were considered better able to fight. With the poorer tenants the landlord was quite willing to settle, and did settle. Ultimately the landlord offered to take two-thirds of a year's rent in discharge of all rent due from each tenant; but the Plan insisted on more, so the landlord was driven to exercise his legal rights. Twenty-four tenants were evicted. These held 1,026 statute acres at an annual rental of £626. They owed £2,406. The landlord's offer was to forgive £1,469 altogether. He asked for £459 at once, £459 before the end of the year, and £50 costs—in all, £939—in discharge of a debt of £2,406. The landlord having received *no rent at all* from March 31st, 1885, up to May, 1889, at last capitulated. What was called an "arbitration" was resorted to, to cover his retreat.

The Olphert Estate.

On this estate were 460 tenants, of whom 220 had judicial rents. The estate was wiped clear of all arrears by the Act of 1882. Mr. Olphert has always resided with his tenants, never sleeping off his estate. He never had any trouble with them until the League was formed. In July, 1884, he evicted 32 tenants, who, however, paid up and were reinstated. For more than two years prior to the recent evictions no rent was paid. The Plan of Campaign was adopted and an all round reduction demanded. The landlord offered 25 per cent. to non-judicial tenants and 10 per cent. to those with fair rents, while he asked for *no arrears.* The "fair rent" tenants had also abatements in addition under the Act of 1887, or a reduction of about 33 per cent. The landlord's offer was refused and no rent was paid. Fourteen tenants were evicted—*all with fair rents—fixed by Mr. Pierce Mahony* (now Parnellite M.P.). The poor law valuation of the holdings was £58 10s. 0d., the old rent £69 18s. 6d., and the judicial rent £56 12s. 0d. *Every Protestant tenant settled with the landlord.* The tenant-right on this estate was particularly valuable. Patrick McElroy, rent £2 4s. per annum, sold his tenant-right to John McGinley for £60, while Father McFadden of Gweedore sold his tenant-right in a holding subject to a rent of £1 2s. 6d. per annum for £115! (See Free Sale).

The Kenmare Estate.

This estate is the largest in Ireland, extending over 100,000 acres, and Killarney is its centre. Between 1851 and 1885 Lord Kenmare spent £129,314 out of his own pocket on improvements, and also got £34,500 from the Board of Works for the same purpose, never charging a single tenant a penny interest, though the money was all spent in building, fencing, draining, and the like. Wherever there is a good house, it has been built with Lord Kenmare's money, and the Land Commissioners always reported that the rental was moderate. In August, 1888, everything was comparatively quiet, when the following letter was written to start the Plan of Campaign:—

"Telephone No. 3,070. Telegraphic address, 'Hostelry,' London.

"Confidential.

"Westminster Palace Hotel, Victoria Street, London, S.W.,
"August 25th, 1888.

"My dear Sheehan,—It will be most necessary to show Balfour that his troubles in Ireland are only beginning. We are arranging a series of great demonstrations through Ireland for the latter end of September and beginning of October. You ought to arrange a series of meetings from parish to parish in your division to address your constituents, announcing them publicly. I will, if possible, address some one of them myself. Don't mention my name publicly as suggesting the meetings. You cannot announce too many of them, but one will do, to begin, any Sunday after next.

"Ever yours sincerely,
"WILLIAM O'BRIEN.

"J. D. Sheehan, Esq., M.P."

The Plan was adopted, and a reduction of 40 per cent. demanded. Moonlighting accompanied it, having previously altogether subsided from earlier days. The Plan gradually lingered, and the latest news is that it has altogether collapsed on a large part of the estate, where it was never a voluntary enterprise on the part of the tenants, but was enforced by every species of terrorism. (*See* p. 165.)

The Smith-Barry Estate.

The case of this estate is, perhaps, the latest, as it is certainly the most unique, of all. Mr. Smith-Barry, M.P., had, as has been seen, intervened in the case of the Ponsonby tenants. It has never been alleged for a moment that the rents on his estate were not perfectly fair or that the tenants were unable to pay them. In August, 1889, however, a meeting of the Smith-Barry tenants was held and attended (why?) by Mr. William

O'Brien, M.P. At this meeting resolutions were passed pledging the tenants to assist the campaigners on the Ponsonby estate in Cork; and it was further decided that each of the tenants on Mr. Smith-Barry's estate in Tipperary should pay an assessment amounting to 10 per cent. on the Government valuation of their holdings, to form a fund for the benefit of the Ponsonby tenants. A further resolution was then passed to the effect that, as the voluntary assessment would bear somewhat heavily on the Tipperary tenants, they should demand 25 per cent. off their rents from their landlord, and thus make money by their noble generosity! This being declined, payment was refused, whereupon the landlord went to law to recover his rents. He recovered judgment against 20 tenants; who, in almost every case, at once capitulated and paid their debts. As a result, their windows were smashed and they were boycotted. Having first capitulated to the landlord, these tenants have now been compelled to capitulate to the League, and further conflict is imminent.

Summary of Campaign Estates.

The facts briefly given will indicate the working of the Plan of Campaign. Those, however, who desire further and fuller information will find it in the publications of the Irish Loyal and Patriotic Union dealing with the subject; and, in "Disturbed Ireland," a book by Mr. T. W. Russell, M.P., dealing at length with the Vandeleur, Clanricarde, Olphert, Kenmare, Lewis, Coolgreany, and other estates. What has been here given shows the utter untruth of the following statements:—

(*a*) That the Plan is a combination to help the poor.

(*b*) That it is caused by necessity.

(*c*) That it is caused by "arrears."

(*d*) That it is the offspring of the rejection of Mr. Parnell's Bill of 1886.

A final word may be urged in connection with this last point. Mr. Gladstone, in a speech at Hampstead, has distinctly stated, "The Plan of Campaign sprang out of that rejection." How utterly untrue this is, will be seen at once if it is remembered that Mr. Parnell's Bill proposed to do nothing for the non-judicial tenants, who, nevertheless, have joined actively in the Plan of Campaign. If by the passing of Mr. Parnell's Bill the Plan of Campaign would have been obviated, these non-judicial tenants are now acting with gross dishonesty; if this be not so, the Bill could not have prevented the Plan. On the Luggacurran estate, for instance, not more than two or three tenants could possibly have been affected by Mr. Parnell's Bill, but Mr. William O'Brien, M.P., worked the Plan there on behalf of all the tenants. On the Coolgreany estate, again, 77 tenants would have been utterly unaffected by that Bill, yet 50 of these joined in the Plan, with the encouragement of the entire Nationalist Party.*

In view of these considerations it may be well to notice that the *Daily News*, which was favourable to Mr. Parnell's Bill, spoke thus of the Plan of Campaign: "WE BY NO MEANS APPROVE OF MR. DILLON'S POLICY. HIS 'PLAN OF CAMPAIGN' SEEMS TO US VITIATED WITH DISHONESTY." (*Daily News*, December 6, 1886.)

PROTESTANT TENANTS AND THE PLAN OF CAMPAIGN. It must never be forgotten that, as will have been inferred from the preceding remarks, *not a single Protestant tenant-farmer has been induced to join the Plan of Campaign.* On estate after estate, where the same terms were offered to both Roman Catholics and Protestants, holding farms side by side, the latter have testified to the justice of the law and the dishonesty of the Plan. As a consequence they have, of course, been denounced, as by the Rev. Father Hughes, chairman of the Monasterevan branch of the National League, who is reported in the local organ (the *Leinster Leader*) of December 15th, 1888, as follows:—

* On the fifteen largest estates 10,820 tenants joined the Plan of Campaign, of whom only 2,850 could have been in the least affected by Mr. Parnell's Bill.

Where are the Protestant farmers of this parish? Are they here to-day as they ought to be? No, they are not. . . . *I say they are contemptible dastards, and I say they are imbeciles if they hope that by-and-bye, when the fight is over and the battle won, their refusal to help us shall not be remembered.*

The Real Object of the Irish Land Movement.

It must never be forgotten that the real object of the Irish land movement is to drive out English power from Ireland; it is not a movement to ameliorate the condition of the Irish peasantry, but to extirpate those known as the "English garrison." This fact has never been concealed by the Parnellite members, as the following extracts from speeches will show:—

"I wish to see the tenant-farmers prosperous; but large and important as is the class of tenant-farmers, constituting as they do, with their wives and families, the majority of the people of this country, *I would not have taken off my coat and gone to this work if I had not known that we were laying the foundation in this movement for the regeneration of our legislative independence.*"

Mr. Parnell, at Galway, October 1, 1880.
(*Freeman's Journal* report.)

"We believe that landlordism is the prop of English rule, and we are working to take that prop away. To drive out British rule from Ireland, we must strike at the foundation, and that foundation is landlordism."

Mr. T. M. Healy, at Boston, December 24, 1881.
(*Irishman* report.)

"We wish to get rid of British rule in Ireland. Landlordism is the prop of that rule—it must be abolished."

Mr. T. M. Healy, at New Orleans, February 4, 1882.

"All our action with regard to this intermediary question of the landlords and tenants is only a step towards the great goal of Irish Nationality."

Rev. Mr. Cantwell, P.P., V.F., Dublin, September 23, 1886.

"If they must have any hunting at all, let them keep their hands in practice by hunting landlords. Hunt them up hill and down dale, until landlords are as scarce as foxes."

Mr. William O'Brien, M.P., Carrick-on-Suir,
September 7, 1884.

"I want you to understand that the reduction of rent we require is not a small, or a petty, or a legal reduction, but the total abolition of rent."

MR. T. P. O'CONNOR, St. Louis, U.S.A.
(*United Ireland*, January 28, 1882.)

"Fair rent is an abomination—a crime not alone against modern civilisation, but a crime against common sense, and a blasphemy against God."

REV. EUGENE SHEEHY, New York.
(*Irish World*, December 17, 1881.)

"If they were going to be evicted for non-payment of the entire rents, let them be evicted with their rent in their pockets."

DR. J. E. KENNY, M.P., Dublin, September 29, 1886.

"Nothing can prevent you continuing the glorious work begun by Michael Davitt at Irishtown and exterminating landlordism root and branch, and all its seed, breed, and generation. It has pleased God that our lot has been cast in days when we can enjoy the religious equality, education, political power, and social emancipation that our forefathers sighed for and spilled their blood for in many a hopeless age, and we would be unworthy of our ancestors, we would deserve the scorn and indignation of those that would come after us, if in this day of dawning hope and power for the Irish we ever falter or flinch until we have banished the twin demons of landlordism and of English rule for ever from our shores (cheers), and until we have planted on the highest pinnacle of Dublin Castle the flag of a redeemed and regenerated Irish nation."

MR. W. O'BRIEN, M.P., Tulla, Co. Clare, May 24, 1885.

The foregoing passages—and there are many others—which may be found in a volume already alluded to ("As It was Said," published by the Irish Loyal and Patriotic Union), may be relied on to prove—

1. That the attack on the landlords is not a *bonâ fide* attack in consequence of their conduct, but an attack against them because they are loyal to Great Britain.

2. That landlords—just or unjust—are to be extirpated in view of this political end.

3. That "fair" rent is not what is desired.

These considerations will of course be supplemented by details drawn from the Plan of Campaign cases. The following facts will also exemplify what has been said :—

A. The policy of the Plan of Campaign was really invented in the year 1848 by an Irish rebel of the period—one Finton Lalor—who recommended its adoption in the pages of the *Irish Felon*, not because the landlords were unjust, but because it was the best means of striking a blow against England. Mr. Michael Davitt has proclaimed the identity of Parnellite views with those of Finton Lalor. On the 23rd of January, 1887, he spoke at New York, using the following words :—" *What are the doctrines of the Irish Revolution? I will quote* what they are from the columns of a paper which bore a very suggestive title, the *Irish Felon*. In the *Felon* of June 24th, 1848, Finton Lalor not only laid down the doctrine of 'The Land for the People,' but also indicated the means by which a movement on these lines would ultimately achieve Irish National Independence." The Young Irelanders of 1848 rejected Lalor's proposal of a strike against all rent; so did the Fenian party of 1866; so did Mr. Butt's party; but it has been adopted by the Parnellites. (For a full description of the past history of this movement, *see* "The Continuity of the Irish Revolutionary Movement," by Professor Brougham Leech, published by Ridgway & Co., price threepence.)

B. The policy of the Campaigners is also evidenced by the fact that a Parnellite landlord is never denounced, even if he be a far higher rent-charger than a Loyalist. The following case will prove instructive:—

The Corporation of Dublin is a body composed of 60 members. Its political complexion is undoubted, 55 of its members being Parnellites—5 being Parnellite M.P.'s, and the Lord Mayor being Mr. Sexton, M.P. They have agricultural tenants who are made to pay every penny of rent, and who never are allowed—under pain of eviction—to get into arrears. In the last week of September, 1888, the Land Commissioners proceeded to fix fair rents for certain tenants of this Corporation at Baldoyle with the following results:—

Name of Tenant.	Area of Holding.			Government Valuation.			Old Rent.			New Rent.			Rductn. per cent.
	A.	R.	P.	£	s.	d.	£	s.	d.	£	s.	d.	
Michael Donnelly	30	1	6	39	0	0	70	0	0	46	0	0	35½
Thomas Duffy	83	1	4	127	0	0	178	12	6	141	0	0	21½
Richard Howison	84	2	27	140	0	0	161	13	0	122	0	0	24½
Nicholas Kearns	70	3	18	100	15	0	129	14	0	112	0	0	13
Patrick Peakin	64	0	0	90	0	0	135	0	0	105	0	0	23
John Rafter	94	1	6	128	15	0	208	16	10	157	0	0	24½
Total	427	1	21	625	10	0	883	16	4	683	0	0	23

It will be observed that in these cases the rent was (1) over £2 an acre, vastly in excess of the average; (2) 41 per cent. over the Government valuation; and (3) reduced by the Land Commissioners A VAST DEAL MORE PER CENT. THAN WERE THE RENTS OF LORD CLANRICARDE'S TENANTS, yet no one ever dreams of denouncing this Corporation as *rack-renters.* Politics forbid.

THE LAND-GRABBER.

Boycotting is treated of in its proper place (*see* pp. 166—171). It should be observed, in connection with the Land Question, that one defence, if such it be, is frequently made for it; it has been over and over again declared that boycotting ought to be enforced against "land-grabbers." This being so, it is important to recollect who the "land-grabber" is. He is the man who takes a farm from which another person has been evicted.

At Ennis on September 18, 1880, Mr. Parnell gave special orders that "when a man takes a farm from which another has been evicted" he should be treated "as if he were a leper of old." Many similar directions can be found in Parnellite literature. For example, Dr. Kenny, M.P., has said that "boycotting, as sanctioned by the League, was only boycotting directed against the one great evil—land-grabbing."

The speaker should therefore be prepared to explain to a meeting what a "land-grabber" is. Why should not a man be free to take a farm from which another is evicted? No man will take a farm from which another is unjustly evicted—that is, for non-payment of an unfair rent. The truth is that the Parnellites hate the "land-grabber" because he is the man who can only exist after a perfectly just eviction. He is the man who comes forward and says, "I myself will take the farm at the rent, and make it pay me." He is objected to because he is a living witness to the equity of eviction.

Savings Banks.

It is important that the speaker should be provided with statistics from which to acquaint his audience with facts from which they can calculate the ability of the Irish tenant to pay. The following figures will be found useful:—

England and Wales, increase in ten years (1877–87)			74 per cent.	
Scotland	,,	,,	,,	108 ,,
Ireland	,,	,,	,,	121 ,,

In the Post Office Savings Banks and the Trustee Savings Banks, being the banks used by artisans, agricultural labourers, and small farmers, we find that in 1879 the deposits amounted to £3,490,000; but in 1888 to £5,140,000—an increase of nearly 50 per cent.

The following table gives the total amount invested in Government Stocks, Joint Stock Banks, Trustee Savings Banks, and Post Office Savings Banks, at intervals, for the last decade. They point to a falling-off where landlords invest, and a rapid increase in the investments of tenants:—

Invested in Government Stock.		Deposits in			Total.	Amount per head.
		Post Office.	Trustee Savings Banks.	Joint Stock Banks.		
1880	£33,113,000	£1,481,000	£2,063,000	£29,350,000	£66,007,000	£12·68
1882	31,772,000	1,832,000	2,038,000	30,667,000	63,309,000	12·41
1884	30,859,000	2,150,000	2,072,000	30,072,000	65,153,000	13·13
1886	30,484,000	2,592,000	1,994,000	29,223,000	64,293,900	13·15
1888	28,856,000	3,128,000	2,012,000	30,310,000	64,306,000	13·45

The following figures are from Mr. Hurlbert's book, entitled "Ireland under Coercion." They are taken from the official returns and show the amount due to depositors in a series of towns in the most disturbed districts in Ireland :—

Office.	1880. £	s.	d.	1887. £	s.	d.	Increase per cent.
Falcarragh	62	15	10	494	10	8	698
Killorglin	282	15	9	1,299	2	6	396
Mitchelstown	1,387	13	2	2,846	9	3	104
Six-Mile-Bridge ...	382	17	10	934	13	4	144
Woodford	259	14	6	1,350	17	11	421
Youghal	3,031	0	7	7,038	7	2	131

SUMMARY.

How the Land Laws of Ireland stand may be conjectured by Radicals from the following words of the Right Hon. John Morley, M.P., spoken at Chelmsford on January 7th, 1886 :—"The late Government, to their great honour, passed an Act to prevent landlords confiscating the property of their tenants. That was a noble exploit. I do not think we shall be able to deal satisfactorily with Ireland until we have passed some legislation to prevent tenants confiscating the property of their landlords."

Part III.

"COERCION."

EVERY accusation levelled by the Parnellite Party against the present Government, or against the Unionist Party, may be referred to one or other of three main heads. These are:—

A. An attack on the Unionist Party for having brought in a Bill which makes the law in Ireland different from the law in England in any respect. It is tacitly assumed very often that this means inequality of treatment, and therefore merits the term "Coercion."

B. An attack, or attacks, on the provisions or supposed provisions of the Crimes Act of 1887, which are often alleged to be tyrannical, and therefore to merit the term "Coercion."

C. Lastly, attacks are made, not on the law, but on its administration, which is alleged to be peculiarly unjust. It is stated frequently that the men who are prosecuted and punished ought not to be prosecuted or punished, and that the treatment they receive is in itself tyrannical, and therefore merits the term "Coercion."

It will be found, on examination, that every alleged case of hardship mentioned by the Parnellites or their English and Scotch allies falls naturally under one or other of these heads. As Unionists insist that the state of Ireland rendered a

Crimes Act necessary, that the Crimes Act itself is in no sense tyrannical, and that the right men have been convicted and punished under its provisions, it is convenient to examine each of the Parnellite charges in turn.

It should, however, be pointed out, in the first place, especially to voters whose political education is not of the highest order, that, after all,

Coercion is only a Nickname.

There has never been any measure known to Parliament as a Coercion Bill. The term is only an abusive epithet given to a certain class of measures by the speakers and writers of the Irish Party. It has been applied to every measure brought in of late years to facilitate the detection and punishment of Irish outrage and murder, whether Mr. Gladstone or Lord Salisbury happened to introduce it. That this is so will at once be made clear from the following interesting extract from the manifesto of the Home Rule Party issued in November, 1885, and signed by Mr. T. P. O'Connor, M.P. :—

Mr. T. P. O'Connor on the Liberal Party and Coercion.

"The Liberal Party denounced Coercion; and it practised a system of Coercion more brutal than that of any previous administration, Liberal or Tory. Under this system jurors were packed with a shamelessness unprecedented even in Liberal Administrations, *and innocent men were hung*, or sent to the living death of penal servitude. . . . . The last declaration of Mr. Gladstone was that he intended to renew the worst clauses of the Act of 1882, and if our long-delayed triumph had not turned the Liberal Government out of office, Lord Spencer would at this moment be in Dublin Castle, and Coercion would be triumphant in Ireland."

Mr. Parnell on the Liberal Party and Coercion.

The above pronouncement was at once ratified by Mr. Parnell, who on November 22nd, 1885, wrote as follows:—

"With this manifesto I heartily concur. It was drawn up with my sanction and with my approval. . . . The Liberal Party gave us chains, imprisonment, and death."

A.—A CRIMES ACT NECESSARY.

The Unionist Party, however, meet the first line of attack by asserting that a Crimes Act for Ireland became necessary in 1887 owing to the PARALYSIS OF LAW in that country. In support of this contention reference can be made both (1) to the statement of Her Majesty's judges, and (2) to the Criminal Statistics and Returns.

THE EVIDENCE OF THE JUDGES.

On February 28th, 1887, Mr. Justice O'Brien—a judge placed on the bench by Mr. Gladstone—addressed the Grand Jury of the County Clare as follows :—

"All these returns which I have before me, and the information which has reached me from other quarters of an unquestionably authentic character, lead me to the conclusion that *law, to a great extent, has ceased to exist in this county.*"—*Freeman's Journal*, March 1st, 1887.

On March 9th, 1887, Mr. Justice Lawson—Attorney-General under Mr. Gladstone's Government, and placed on the bench by Mr. Gladstone—addressed the Grand Jury of the County Mayo as follows :—

"The present state of things is morally unsatisfactory, and, according to the reports made to me, approaches as near to rebellion against the authority in the country as anything short of civil war can be."—*Irish Times*, March 10th, 1887.

On March 10th, 1887, Mr. Justice O'Brien addressed the Grand Jury of the County Kerry as follows :—

"These returns present a picture of the County of Kerry such as could hardly be found in any country that has passed the confines of natural society, and entered on the duties and relations and acknowledged obligations of civilised life. The law is defeated—perhaps I should rather say has ceased to exist—houses are attacked by night and by day, even the midnight terror yielding to the noonday audacity of crime; person and life are assailed; the terrified inmates are wholly unable to do anything to protect themselves, and a state of terror and lawlessness prevails everywhere."—*Freeman's Journal*, March 11th, 1887.

On March 14th, 1887, Mr. Justice Johnson—Attorney-General under Mr. Gladstone's Government, and placed on the bench by Mr. Gladstone—addressed the Grand Jury of the County Cork as follows:—

"The returns from this and the West Riding—and they cover a period of only three months since the last winter assizes—show that in a considerable portion of this great county the people who live in remote and isolated districts are subject to violence, alarm, and plunder by day and by night—principally by night—from gangs of armed men, disguised mainly, who rove through the country seizing arms, plundering property, always with a show of violence, often accompanied with threats, and sometimes with assaults of the meanest and most dastardly character."—*Daily Express*, March 15th, 1887.

On the same day (March 14th, 1887) Mr. Justice Murphy, also placed on the bench by Mr. Gladstone, addressed the Grand Jury of the County Galway as follows:—

"They" (the officials) "report to me that there is a complete paralysis of law, that it is unable to protect many of the inhabitants in the exercise of their most ordinary rights, and that lawlessness is perfectly supreme."—*Daily Express*, March 15th, 1887.

UNPUNISHED CRIME IN 1886.

In the year 1886 out of 1,025* cases of agrarian offences there were only 64 convictions; out of six cases of murder there was only one conviction; out of forty-three cases of firing into dwellings there were no convictions; and out of seventy-three cases of mutilation of cattle there were no convictions. It was not the allegation of the Unionist Party at any time that cases of crime were terribly numerous; the contention, which the above figures amply prove, was that

* See figures, pp. 152, 153.

life and property were rendered absolutely insecure by the complete immunity from punishment possessed by the perpetrators of these outrages. It was not a question of ordinary crime, but of agrarian crime, committed for a definite object over large tracts of country—a class of crime to which England, Scotland, and Wales afford no parallel.

Why Justice was Paralysed.

The large number of unpunished crimes was, then, the chief reason why the Unionist Party brought in a Crimes Act in 1887. There could, indeed, be little doubt how this paralysis arose. It was caused by (1) the unwillingness of witnesses to give evidence, and (2) the unwillingness of jurors to convict.

Unwilling Witnesses.

The unwillingness of Irish witnesses at all times to give information to the authorities will scarcely be doubted. Quantities of proof that they were unwilling before the introduction of the Crimes Act may be found in the pages of the evidence taken before the Cowper Commission. (*See*, for example, Answers 17,901—17,907 ; 17,279—17,284 ; 17,613—17,615.)

It would, indeed, hardly seem necessary to dwell on this point. If crime be undetected to such an abnormal extent, there must either be scarcity of evidence and reluctant witnesses, or juries afraid or unwilling to act according to their oaths.

Why Witnesses were Unwilling.

There is, however, good reason to know why witnesses were unwilling, and why they must have been reluctant to give evidence. Illustrations of the treatment they received on daring to come forward are not rare. On June 14th, 1885, MR. CASHMAN, a young man of twenty, was beaten to death when walking home from Millstreet, in the County of Cork, because he was suspected of giving information to the police. On September 19th, 1885, THOMAS DEANE, of Dysart, Corofin, was visited by Moonlighters, who wounded him in the leg because he had given information to some sheriffs' bailiffs. On October 30th, 1886, MR. MICHAEL ROCHE KELLY was shot for giving evidence at the Ennis Licensing Sessions. The well-known case of NORAH FITZMAURICE, boycotted because she dared to give evidence against her father's murderers, is another excellent illustration of what witnesses in Ireland may expect.

Unwilling Jurors.

That jurors in Ireland were unwilling to convict in many cases will scarcely be doubted. Plenty of evidence to prove their reluctance will also be found in the Report of the Cowper Commission already alluded to. (*See* Answers 18,571 —18,605.)

At the Clare and Limerick Assizes, March, 1887 (presided over by Mr. Justice O'Brien and Mr. Justice Johnson respectively) the criminal business came to an abrupt termination in consequence of repeated failures of justice in the cases already tried. At Clare the Crown declined to proceed further, whereupon the judge said :—

> "Having regard to the verdicts in the two cases yesterday, my opinion—my fixed opinion—is that nothing but an entire failure of justice can take place."

At Limerick, owing to persistent verdicts of acquittal, the judge was asked to adjourn the assizes, which he at once did.

Why Jurors were Unwilling.

The following facts, however, will not only show why jurors were unwilling, but will also show that they must have been reluctant :—

By the orders of Captain Moonlight (see *Kerry Evening Post*—a Nationalist paper—of January 29th, 1887) two Cork butter merchants, who had recently served as jurors—DOMINICK CRONIN and TERENCE MCMAHON by name—were ordered to be boycotted. "If you do not do as requested, and boycott these tools of the Crown, you will be COERCED into doing so." So ran the proclamation.

How popular feeling ran in Ireland with reference to jurors may be tested by the following extract from *United Ireland* of December 4th, 1886:—

> "There is no word of secrecy in the oath. The grand jurors (it may be in the interests of genteel jobbery) pledge themselves that 'their fellow-jurors' counsel they shall not disclose.' The petit juror binds himself by no such pledge. The marked omission of the words would seem in itself an express denial of the existence of such an obligation of silence, and it may well be that the white light of public opinion, and the hot fire of public odium, is the best remedy for the monstrous abuses that have sprung up in the jury-box under the shelter of the judicially imposed darkness. The most besotted and bloodthirsty juror will, we fancy, moderate his eagerness for conviction, if he knows there is a right of appeal from the dark security of the jury-box to the calm judgment of his neighbours in the world outside."

These words undoubtedly seem to indicate that the juror who dared to be for conviction was to be reported by other jurors and punished. Whether this view is correct the sequel will show, as the article from which we have quoted evoked an indignant protest from a Mr. T. W. Rolleston, a well-known Home Ruler, who wrote as follows to Mr. William O'Brien, M.P., *editor*:—

> "Your proposal to reveal the names of the convicting jurymen, who, it is to be presumed, will be Protestants, makes me ask myself the question, painful enough to one of my political sympathies, 'Do the assurances we have received that our liberties will be respected by our Catholic fellow-citizens in a free Ireland, mean anything more than that we shall be let alone if in our civic and political actions we take care never to run counter to the dominant spirit of the time and place?'"

To this protest the editor of *United Ireland* replied :—

"In a selfgoverned Ireland it would, of course, be intolerable that men should not be allowed to differ freely in the jury-box and everywhere else; but in the state of chaotic conflict to which English rule reduces it, he who is not with us is against us, and must expect to be dealt with accordingly."

These words show, beyond yea or nay, the fact that the Parnellites contended that jurors must, if necessary, break their oaths, lest they should help the Government by finding a conviction.

"Coercion" the only Alternative to Home Rule.

It should never be forgotten for a moment that, as a matter of history and fact, *the entire responsibility* for the Crimes Act of 1886 rests on the shoulders of the Parnellite Party.

Speaking at Glenbrien, County Wexford, on December 5th, 1886, this fact was confessed and gloried in by Mr. John E. Redmond, M.P., who spoke as follows :—

"When Mr. Gladstone was defeated in England last year, and when the Tories came into power, they boasted they could govern Ireland by means of the ordinary law. Mr. Gladstone, on the contrary, told the people of England that they had to choose between 'Coercion' on the one side, and Home Rule on the other. Home Rule was defeated at the last election in Great Britain, and I say advisedly that if in the face of that defeat the Tories had been able to rule Ireland with the ordinary law the result would have been, in England and Scotland, to throw back our cause, perhaps for a generation, and to give the lie direct to the prophecy of Mr. Gladstone. . . . We have been able to force the Government to give up the ordinary law and to fall back once more on 'Coercion.'" —*Enniscorthy Guardian* (Nationalist paper), Dec. 11th, 1886.

The above speech clearly proves—

1. *That Coercion was not a necessary sequel to the refusal to grant Home Rule.*
2. *That Coercion was forced on by the Parnellites for political ends.*

SUMMARY.

The foregoing facts and extracts will supply those requiring them with the means of defending the Unionist Party against any charge of having wantonly or recklessly brought in a Crimes Bill. Should further particulars be required they will be found in the section entitled "THE REAL COERCION" (p. 164).

B.—THE CRIMES ACT OF 1887.

ITS PROVISIONS.

What, then, were the provisions of the Crimes Act of 1887? The following is a full and accurate synopsis of the clauses of that measure; but speakers are earnestly advised to have a copy of the Act always with them for reference :—

Section 1 provides for a preliminary inquiry upon oath when a crime has been committed, but before any person is charged with its commission.*

Section 2 provides that "any person who shall commit *any of the following offences*" may be prosecuted before a Court of Summary Jurisdiction (*see* Sect. 5) :—

Offences.

1. Taking "part in any criminal conspiracy *now punishable by law.*"
2. Wrongfully and without legal authority using violence and intimidation.

* A similar law exists in Scotland.

3. Taking part in any riot or *unlawful assembly.*
4. Taking forcible possession of premises from which any one has been evicted within twelve months previous.
5. Assaulting or obstructing officers of the law.
6. Inciting any person to commit the above offences.*

Section 3 provides that where recourse is not had to a Court of Summary Jurisdiction, a Special Jury may be had on application by the Crown or the defendant.

Section 4 provides that if the Attorney-General believes a fair trial cannot be had in a certain county, the Court shall order the trial to be had in some other county named by him.†

Section 5 provides that the Lord-Lieutenant may proclaim certain districts for the purposes of the Act. Until he so proclaims them there can be no Court of Summary Jurisdiction, as in Sect. 2, save for the punishment of offence No. 3—viz., taking part in any riot or unlawful assembly.

Section 6 provides for a special proclamation by the Lord-Lieutenant of dangerous associations. Before proclaiming any association, however, he must be satisfied that it is—

(*a*) Formed for the commission of crimes; or

(*b*) Carrying on operations for or by the commission of crimes; or

(*c*) Encouraging or aiding persons to commit crimes; or

(*d*) Promoting or inciting to acts of violence or intimidation; or

* It will be observed that the Act does not make these things offences. It only provides that these things, which are and always have been offences in England and Scotland, as well as Ireland, shall be tried by a Court of Summary Jurisdiction.

† The Lord Advocate—Attorney-General for Scotland—has this power.

(*e*) Interfering with the administration of the law; or disturbing the maintenance of law and order.

The Lord-Lieutenant cannot act in this without the advice of the Privy Council. His proclamation must be laid before Parliament within seven days if it be sitting, or within seven days after its meeting, and within fourteen days either House of Parliament can address the Crown. In this section the word "crime" means "felony," "misdemeanour," or any of the offences specified in Section 2 or 7.

Section 7 provides for the suppression of any association deemed to be "dangerous," as defined in Section 6. When it is proclaimed, it becomes an unlawful association; and those who take part in its meetings, or publish its proceedings, "*with a view to promote*" *its* "*objects*," are guilty of an offence under the Act.*

Section 8 renews the Peace Preservation (Ireland) Act of 1881, amended in 1886 so as to make it legal to search for arms or ammunition in proclaimed districts.

Sections 9 and 10 are sections of procedure.

Section 11 limits punishment before a Court of Summary Jurisdiction to six months, and gives the same right of appeal possessed by all persons brought up under the common law in England or Ireland before such Courts—that is, an appeal if the sentence be more than one month.

It also provides that every such Court must be a Court of *two* resident magistrates, one of whom shall be a person of the sufficiency of whose "legal knowledge the Lord-Lieutenant shall be satisfied."

It also provides an appeal at quarter sessions to the County Court judge.

Sections 12, 13, 14, and 15 are concerned merely with matters of form.

* The words in italics are most material.

Section 16 provides that no one can be punished twice for the same offence.

Section 18 provides that "an agreement or combination which, under the Trades' Union Act, 1871 and 1876, or the Conspiracy and Protection of Property Act, 1875, is legal, shall not, nor shall any act done in pursuance of any such agreement or combination, be deemed to be an offence against the provisions of this Act respecting conspiracy, intimidation, and dangerous associations."

Sections 17, 19 and 20 are merely formal.

PARNELLITE FICTIONS ABOUT THE CRIMES ACT.

The following is a carefully selected list of some of the current Parnellite untruths about the provisions of the Act :—

1. *That the Act creates new offences. Answer:* (1) This may be true *technically*, because on appeal an offence may be described as an offence against the Act itself, which of course could not be before it was passed; but, *practically*, it is utterly untrue. (2) Assuming it, however, to be true that new offences are created, how is it Parnellites cannot tell the section, part of section, or word in the Act that creates the new offence?

2. *That the Act alters the law of conspiracy in Ireland so that what is not punishable in England is punishable in Ireland. Answer:* This is utterly untrue. The Act is explicit; the criminal conspiracy must be one which, at the date of the passing of the Act, was already punishable by law. (Sect. 2.)

3. *That the Lord-Lieutenant can stop public meetings in*

Ireland. Answer: He can only proclaim meetings of associations which are dangerous under the definitions of Section 6. Of course he has also the right—not under this Act, but at common law—to prohibit all meetings likely to result in riot or breach of the peace, or held for an illegal object. This is also law in England and Scotland.

4. *That the press can be suppressed, and innocent newsvendors arrested. Answer:* This is quite impossible. No one can be touched under Section 7 unless he acts "with a view to promote the objects" of a dangerous association. The intent of a newsvendor, for example, *must be proved.*

5. *That the Courts of Summary Jurisdiction are not competent. Answer:* Each Court must consist of two magistrates, one of whom is a trained lawyer, of whose knowledge the Lord-Lieutenant (*i.e.*, in practice the Lord Chancellor, who advises the Crown) must be satisfied. The trained lawyer must concur in the decision.

6. *That prisoners are defrauded in Ireland of the right of appeal. Answer:* This is quite untrue; they have all the rights they have in England.

7. *That what is punished in Ireland is what is often permitted in England when done by Trades' Unions. Answer:* How utterly untrue this is, the words of Section 18 fully prove. (*See* preceding page.)

There are many other Parnellite fictions about the Crimes Act, but the best method of meeting them is by an accurate knowledge of the terms of the Act.

The Crimes Act of 1887 and Scotch Law.

Notwithstanding what has been said, the speaker will find himself continually questioned by persons who contend that in consequence of the operation of the Crimes Act, *which is not in force in England*, Ireland is coerced.

It is not denied that the Crimes Act has altered Irish law. Before it passed, the law in Ireland, as regards crime, was identical with the law in England. Since the Crimes Act was passed, that is no longer so. Nothing which was not crime before has been made crime, but the method of dealing with crime has been altered. There has undoubtedly been *a difference of procedure.*

This very fact is fastened on every day as an Irish grievance. There is, however, one excellent and conclusive answer ready at hand. The methods of the Crimes Act are, and for hundreds of years have been, in force in Scotland. If these methods coerce Ireland, Scotland also must be a coerced country.

The following points illustrate the identity of the Irish Crimes Act with Scotch law:—

1. *Preliminary Investigations with regard to Crime.* The Irish members call these "Star Chamber inquiries," but they are in constant use in Scotland. Witnesses are continually examined in private in Scotland by the Procurator Fiscal, who takes down in writing their precognitions or depositions. If they decline to give information, they are examined on oath before the sheriff. If they still decline, they are committed to prison for contempt. This is called "coercion" in Ireland; *if it is, it must also be coercion in Scotland.* Coercion, after all, can hardly be a matter of latitude or longitude.

2. *Summary Jurisdiction.* The crimes which are tried by a Summary Court in Ireland can also be tried by a Summary Court in Scotland. In fact, in case of any difficulty or disturbance in Scotland, the Lord Advocate, an officer who corresponds to the Attorney-

General in England or Ireland, has the undoubted power, *of his own motion*, of directing whether the offence shall be tried with or without a jury. In 1885 and 1886, under Mr. Gladstone's Government, cases were summarily tried at Stornoway, Portree, and Lochmaddy, which in a normal state of public feeling would have been tried by a jury. As regards the constitution of the Summary Court—in Ireland there are two magistrates, in Scotland one sheriff or sheriff substitute. As regards appeal—in Ireland there is an appeal *on the facts* from any sentence exceeding one month, and an appeal on a law-point in every case. In Scotland there is no appeal at all, except on questions of law. This state of affairs is called "coercion" in Ireland; *if it is, there must also be coercion in Scotland.*

3. *Removal of Trial.* In Scotland the Lord Advocate, as Public Prosecutor, has almost unlimited power of fixing the place of trial; it is a matter of continual practice in Scotland. For example, from 1880 to 1887 whole batches of Crofters were brought 300 miles and tried by a jury drawn from the Lothians. This is called "coercion" in Ireland; *if so, Scotland must also be coerced.*

4. *Proclamation of Districts.* It will have been observed that in Ireland the Crimes Act in its main provisions is not of general application; it is only to be put in force in exceptional circumstances. But the procedure we have been considering applies to all Scotland and at all times. This may be "coercion" in Ireland, but *if so, Scotland is far more coerced.*

Justice of the Crimes Act.

What has been said will fully demonstrate the absurdity of those who contend that anything must be "coercion" which is not law in England. The following questions may, however, be justly asked :—

1. What is there unjust or harsh in asking for information upon oath about a crime before any one is charged?

2. What is unjust or harsh in trying prisoners before a Summary Court when trial by jury has broken down?

3. What is unjust or harsh in punishing "taking part in a criminal conspiracy now punishable by law," or intimidation, or violence, or riot, or assault, or incitement to these?

Similarly, a speaker may well go through the Crimes Act of 1887, clause by clause, and demand of his opponents what it is that is really oppressive in each clause, utterly apart from whether it is law in England or Scotland.

MR. GLADSTONE'S COERCION OF 1882.

It may be convenient to compare here, in parallel columns, the provisions of the two Crimes Acts—viz., the Prevention of Crimes Act (passed by Mr. Gladstone in 1882) and the Criminal Law and Procedure Act of the present Government.

Mr. Gladstone's Act of 1882.	The Act of 1887.
Sects. 1, 2, and 3 provide for a Special Commission Court to try treason, murder, arson, attacks on dwelling-houses, &c. The Commission to consist of judges without a jury, and to have powers of life and death.	No such provision.
Sects. 4 and 5 provide for Special Juries in criminal cases.	As in Section 3.
Sect. 6 provides for "change of venue" of trial.	As in Section 4.

Mr. Gladstone's Act of 1882.	The
Sect. 7 defines intimidation, and declares that whoever is guilty of it is guilty of an offence against the Act.	As in Section 2
Sect. 8.—Every one who in a proclaimed district takes part in riot, forcible re-entry, assault or obstruction of officers of the law, is guilty of an offence against the Act.	As in Section 2.
Sect. 9.—Every one who knowingly is a member of an unlawful association, or takes part in its operations, is guilty of an offence.	As in Section 7.*
Sect. 10.—The Lord-Lieutenant may prohibit any meeting which he has reason to believe to be dangerous to the public peace or the public safety.	No such provision
Sect. 11.—Persons out of their house one hour later than sunset or before sunrise may be arrested by a constable on suspicion, and if a Court of Summary Jurisdiction *thinks* he was not on lawful business, it may sentence him to three months' imprisonment.	No such provision.
Sect. 12 provides for the arrest of strangers found under suspicious circumstances.	No such provision.
Sect. 13 provides that the Lord-Lieutenant may seize any newspaper.	No such provision

* Saving that Section 7 of the Act of 1887 goes further in the direction of protecting the offender.

Mr. Gladstone's Act of 1882.	The Act of 1887.
Sect. 14 provides for searching for arms and illegal documents.	No such provision.
Sect. 15 applies this Act to aliens.	No such provision.
Sect. 16 provides for preliminary inquiry.	Section 1.
Sect. 17 provides for apprehension of absconding witnesses.	No such provision.
Sect. 18 provides for additional constabulary force.	No such provision.
Sect. 19.—Power of Lord-Lieutenant to give compensation in cases of murder, maiming, &c.	No such provision
Sect. 21.—Any person guilty of an offence against the Act is liable to six months with or without hard labour from a Summary Court.	*See* Section 2.
Sect. 22 provides for a Summary Court of two resident magistrates.	As in Section 2.
Sect. 23 provides for the proclamation of districts by the Lord-Lieutenant.	As in Section 6.
Sect. 32 excludes Trades' Unions.	As in Section 18.
Sect. 33.—Saving for associations which act "by such means as are not unlawful."	Such associations cannot be so included. (*See* Section 6.)
Sect. 34 defines unlawful associations as those— (*a*) formed for commission of crimes; (*b*) carrying on operations for or by commission of crimes;	

Mr. Gladstone's Act of 1882.	The Act of 1887
(*c*) encouraging or aiding persons to commit crimes.	
Crimes being offences against this Act and indictable offences.	*See* Section 6.

Mr. Parnell's Coercion Bill.

It is well to remind those who talk of "Coercion" that in 1882 Mr. Parnell himself was willing to agree to the introduction of a "Coercion Bill." This statement has been made by Captain O'Shea, ex-M.P. for Galway, and corroborated by the Right Hon. Joseph Chamberlain (see *Times*, August 2, 1888), and *it has never been denied by Mr. Parnell.*

The Results of the Crimes Act.

What, however, have been the results of the Crimes Act, and indeed of previous acts for the same purpose? The following table is taken from the official returns presented to Parliament :—

Official Return of Agrarian Crime.

In the year 1879 the Agrarian Crimes were	870
In the year 1880 they rose to	2,585
In the year 1881 they rose to	4,439
In the first six months of 1882 they rose to	2,597

On the 12th July, 1882, the Prevention of Crimes Act (Mr. Gladstone) Passed.

Result.

In the last six months of 1882 the Agrarian Crimes fell to	836
In the year 1883 they fell to	834
In the year 1884 they fell to	744
From January to June, 1885, they fell to	373

ON THE 12TH JULY, 1885, THE PREVENTION OF CRIMES ACT EXPIRED.

Result.

From July to December, 1885, Agrarian Crimes rose to	543
In the year 1886 (being the year of Mr. Gladstone's so-called "Message of Peace") they mounted up to	1,025
In the first six months of 1887 they were	470

IN JULY, 1887, THE CRIMES ACT (MR. BALFOUR) PASSED.

Result.

In the last six months of 1887 they fell to	399
In the year 1888 they fell to	635
In the first six months of 1889 they fell to	270

The following table gives another practical view of the effects of so-called "Coercion" on crime. It gives the returns for Clare and Kerry for a series of years :—

Year.	Outrages in Clare.	Outrages in Kerry.	Total.	Remarks.
1877 ...	5	8	13	No Agitation.
1878 ...	8	5	13	
1879 ...	21	13	34	Land League begun.
1880 ...	91	298	389	
1881 ...	213	401	614	
1882 ...	207	347	554	Mr. Gladstone's Crimes Act begun.
1883 ...	55	146	201	Crimes Act in full work. Crime reduced.
1884 ...	38	117	155	
1885 ...	88	180	268	Crimes Act ceased. Crime increased.
1886 ...	141	209	350	No Crimes Act. Matters worse.
1887 ...	153	108	261	Crimes Act begun.
1888 ...	104	99	203	Crimes Act working. Crime reduced.

These tables surely demonstrate the efficiency of the Crimes Act of 1887; and it may be added that while in October, 1887, there were 306 persons boycotted in Clare and 477 in Kerry—in all 783—on the first day of January, 1889, there were only 8 in Clare and 34 in Kerry, 42 in all.

C. THE ADMINISTRATION OF IRISH GOVERNMENT.

Quite apart from attacks on the Crimes Act, attacks are made daily on the administration of the law and of the Government in Ireland. Chief among these come the attacks continually made on the Chief Secretary for Ireland. It must not be forgotten that the Chief Secretary is bound to enforce every law passed by the Imperial Parliament, and that it is not a matter of option with him whether Mr. Dillon, Mr. O'Brien, or any other member of Parliament who breaks the law, should be prosecuted or not.

In the case of almost every Irish prisoner it is of late customary to hear four distinct pleas brought forward. These pleas are:—

1. That it is a shame to arrest the leaders of the Irish people.
2. That they only committed a political offence.
3. That they only broke a bad and coercive law.
4. That they are badly treated in prison, having to associate with criminals.

1. To the first of these pleas the obvious answer is that all depends upon what they were doing. The doctrine of class privilege was never asserted in a more odious shape than when it is asserted that members of Parliament, or priests, or Lord Mayors, or editors of newspapers, are to become privileged classes, superior to the law.

2. To the second plea the answer is that it arises from a confusion of ideas. To break the law for political purposes is not necessarily a political offence, nor does an offence become political because it is committed by a politician. On such a principle it might be argued that the Phœnix Park murderers merely committed a political offence.

3 To the third plea, the answer is that no individual can be allowed to choose for himself what laws are good and what bad. If Home Rulers may break laws they think bad which are passed when a Unionist majority is in power, it will be allowable for Irish Loyalists to break laws they consider bad when passed either by Mr. Gladstone or Mr. Parnell. If such a principle be admitted, society must come to an end, and anarchy begin.

4 With regard to the fourth plea, it is monstrous to hear persons pretending that the sacred person of John Dillon or of William O'Brien should not be sent to a common gaol, while the poor peasant who has only obeyed the orders they have given him has to go there. It may also be pointed out that this plea is only raised for party ends. No Gladstonian expressed any sympathy with Mr. Cunninghame Grahame, M.P., when he was obliged to go to prison last year.

IRISH PRISON RULES.

It should also be remembered that the Irish Prison Rules (disciplinary) were settled in 1878. They were approved by Parliament, and were examined and reported on by the Commission of 1884. Part of the reference to that Commission was "the points of difference at present existing between England and Ireland, and the desirability of rendering the two prison systems as nearly as may be uniform."

The Commissioners included Dr. Sigerson, of Dublin (Nationalist), Dr. Robert M'Donnell, of Dublin (Home Ruler), and Mr. T. A. Dickson, now a Parnellite M.P. They made *a unanimous report* in August, 1884, and on the 20th of March following, Mr. Campbell-Bannerman, M.P. (then Chief Secretary), stated in the House of Commons that the recommendations of the Commission had been carried into effect.

The Dietary Rules in England and Ireland are similar,

except that in England no milk is included, while in Ireland, for a prisoner on second-class diet, two pints of new milk are allowed three days a week, and eight ounces of extra bread on the other days. As far as any difference exists it is altogether in favour of Irish prisoners, and if this were not so Mr. Gladstone and Mr. Campbell-Bannerman would alone be responsible.

Parnellite Methods of Dealing with Crimes Act Cases.

There is a familiar Parnellite method of dealing with cases under the Crimes Act, strictly analogous to that pursued by them in reference to evictions—that is, to create an effect by the wholesale suppression of essential facts. For example, diaries and lists of Coercion are published in which cases appear as follows:—

A.B. ... For making a speech ... Three months' imprisonment.

It will be noted that in this familiar form every fact is omitted; and it should be borne in mind that no man can be prosecuted in England, Scotland, or *Ireland* for making a speech, though he can be in any of the three kingdoms for what he says in the speech, should he counsel violence or incite to crime. In view of some of the extraordinary stories disseminated by the Parnellite Party, it may be as well to state here precisely the charges for which some of the Parnellite members of Parliament have been imprisoned under the Crimes Act:—

William O'Brien, M.P. ...	Inciting others to break the law.
T. D. Sullivan, M.P.... ...	Publishing reports of a dangerous association with the view of promoting its objects.
Edward Harrington, M.P. ...	Ditto, ditto.
David Sheehy, M.P.... ...	Inciting persons to resist police in the discharge of their duty.

Alderman Hooper, M.P. ...	... Publishing reports of a dangerous association with the view of promoting its objects.
J. R. Cox, M.P. ...	... Taking part in an unlawful assembly,* *i.e.*, unlawful under the common law.
Patrick O'Brien, M.P.	... Taking part in a criminal conspiracy "now punishable by law" to compel and induce people not to fulfil their legal obligations.
Douglas Pyne, M.P....	... Inciting persons to obstruct officers of the law in discharge of their duty.
J. C. Flynn, M.P. ...	... Criminal conspiracy punishable before the Crimes Act passed.
J. Gilhooly, M.P. ...	... Intimidation.
J. Dillon, M.P. ...	... Inciting persons not to fulfil their legal obligations.

The above list may prove useful, and may suggest the question, What would be done to these members of Parliament, or to English and Scotch members of Parliament, if they acted similarly on the British side of St. George's Channel? Every other imprisoned Parnellite member has been arrested for some offence precisely similar to those in the above list.

* An unlawful assembly is an assembly of three or more persons—

(*a*) With intent to commit a crime by open force; or

(*b*) With intent to carry out any common purpose, lawful or unlawful, in such a manner as to give those courageous persons in the neighbourhood of such assembly reasonable ground to apprehend a breach of the peace in consequence of it.

Parnellite Fictions about Coercion.

Within the limits of this book it is only possible to suggest general lines of argument. It is quite impossible to do more than illustrate the methods of the Parnellite Party. In order to do this, two or three of the more transparent fictions will be briefly dealt with.

The Mandeville Fiction.

It has been alleged by scores of Gladstonian and Parnellite speakers that the late Mr. Mandeville was killed by the treatment he received in prison. The following brief record of the sworn facts, in the teeth of which this false story was manufactured, will be useful :—

On October 31, 1887, Mr. Mandeville was sent to prison, when he weighed 17 stone; on the following Christmas Eve he was released, and then he weighed 16 stone 11 lbs. On Christmas Day he spoke at Mitchelstown on a bitter winter's night; on New Year's Day, 1888, he addressed a meeting in a snowstorm. Day after day, week after week, he spoke at open-air demonstrations, boasting again and again of his unimpaired health. On January 20th he declared imprisonment had not "knocked a feather out of him." More than two months after his release he said that he never "was in better health in his life," this declaration, like the last, being made at a public meeting. During March and April Mr. Mandeville's life was one of unceasing activity in out-door work, organising and speech-making day after day, staying out often in the rain without greatcoat or umbrella, travelling many miles by rail or road, remaining out till the early hours of the morning, and never complaining of ill-health or seeking for medical advice. For nearly six and a half months this continued. At last, on July 2nd, he drove home one morning at 3 o'clock a.m. On the 5th it became plain that he was suffering from a severe cold which had settled in his throat.

The illness took a malignant form, and on July 8th he died. The next day the Nationalists discovered that he had been killed by the treatment he received in prison, a cry which was kept on long after medical evidence had incontestably demonstrated that the disease of which he died could not have been a week old.

The Mitchelstown Fiction.

The current Mitchelstown fiction is as follows:—The Nationalists were holding a perfectly legal meeting; the Government tried to interfere with them by forcing police through the meeting; the police, being forced to retreat, behaved barbarously, and shot two men. The police were therefore guilty of murder.

Against this fiction, sedulously propagated with a great deal of added colour by Mr. Gladstone, who has probably been in this, as in other cases, deceived by some mendacious correspondent, the following facts should be borne in mind:—

That the Government had a perfect right to have a reporter present; and the police advanced to protect him.

That not a single blow was struck by the police (who only asked the crowd to make way) till after they were attacked by men on horseback with crowds of blackthorns.

That the Nationalist press chronicled with delight the fact that the mob charged after the police, and that their helmets were kicked down the street.

That the meeting, which may (though this is doubtful) have been legal, became illegal when the attack on the police began.

That one constable was kicked and beaten within an inch of his life, and will never be fit for any work again.

The first volley fired by the police, which injured nobody, saved his life.

That the police only fired a second time when men advanced to attack the barracks.

That, if the police were wrong, a verdict of guilty should have been given against the officer who ordered them to fire. No such verdict was returned, even by the hostile coroner's jury; though there was no dispute as to who gave the order.

Finally, that the verdict of the coroner's jury was quashed by the high authority of the Court of Queen's Bench.

The "Cheering" or "Groaning" Fiction.

Scarcely a week elapses in which some absolutely untrue fiction is not sedulously propagated by Home Rule speakers or papers. Very frequently the form chosen is one in which it is made to appear that some man has been imprisoned either for cheering Mr. Gladstone or groaning Mr. Balfour. It is, of course, utterly impossible for anything of the kind to take place, either under the Crimes Act or under the ordinary law. Nothing of the kind has ever taken place, and all these cases are chiefly valuable as useful indications of the mendacity of those who give them to the public. It is perfectly true that men who have cheered Mr. Gladstone or groaned Mr. Balfour have been sent to prison, but not *because* they have so cheered or groaned. If a man assaults an officer of the law and cheers Mr. Gladstone as he does so, he is put in prison for the former part of his conduct, not for the latter. If a man takes part in a drunken row and groans Mr. Balfour, he will very likely be arrested, but his groaning will be quite immaterial. As illustrating the usual way in which this ingenious perversion of the truth is worked, we give the following illustration:—

Sir B. W. Foster, M.P. for the Ilkeston division of Derbyshire, stated at Draycott in that division on Jan. 7th, 1889, that "a boy named Burke was sent to prison for groaning at Mr. Balfour's name." Such was the information Sir B. W. Foster had received and accepted in good faith from some press correspondent. What were the facts?

Thomas Burke, a tramp shoemaker, was arrested and charged before a magistrate for being drunk and disorderly. He was ordered to appear and answer to the charge at the sessions held on January 2nd, 1889. He failed to do so, and accordingly a warrant was issued for his arrest. It was, indeed, incidentally stated before the magistrate that when drunk the prisoner had shouted "To hell with Balfour!" but this circumstance had not the most remote connection with his prosecution.

This very recent case is given because there were in the past twelve months at least twenty-five similar cases equally perverted for party ends by suppression and misrepresentation of the actual circumstances.

The Kinsella Fiction.

Kinsella was shot dead in September, 1887, on the occasion of a seizure of tenant's cattle. A coroner's jury found that he was murdered by an emergency man called Freeman, and included in their verdict as guilty of the murder the land agent, Mr. Hamilton, who was admitted at the time to have been in Belfast, 150 miles away. Freeman was not subsequently tried for murder, and so the Government have been accused of screening him.

The following facts will show the value to be placed on this Parnellite tragedy. It was proved in Court, and not disputed, that Freeman's revolver had never been discharged at all; and that the bullet found in Kinsella's body was so large that it never could have been in the revolver. For this and other reasons equally strong, the grand jury threw out the bill, and Freeman was not tried. However, six other emergency men were tried for manslaughter; no juror was ordered by the

Crown to stand aside; twelve tenant farmers were empanelled in the County Wicklow; and the prisoners were acquitted.

The "Laughing" or "Smiling" Fiction.

On March 8th, 1889, the *Leeds Mercury* gave currency to this fiction in the following form:—"Mr. J. S. Dunleavy, editor of the *Clare Independent*, was recently sentenced to three months' imprisonment. This was the charge—'Obstructing a policeman by laughing at him.' And this is how Mr. Dunleavy is treated in prison—'He is confined in a flag cell without matting. His application for furniture has been refused by the Visiting Committee. His sleeping accommodation is a hammock. The rest of the furniture is a stool."

In all this there was not a *syllable of truth*. Proceedings were taken against Mr. Dunleavy under the ordinary law, not for laughing at a policeman, but for conduct calculated to lead to a breach of the peace in unlawfully abusing a police constable while in the execution of his duty. He was ordered to find bail to keep the peace and be of good behaviour. This he refused to do, electing to go to prison for three months. He was treated in prison under the rules for prisoners awaiting trial, and he was, on his application, granted permission to furnish his cell, to receive certain daily and weekly publications, permission to write, the use of books, and permission to smoke twice daily.

In similar fashion the following lie from *United Ireland* was given currency by the *Sheffield Daily Telegraph*. *United Ireland*, February 2nd, 1889: "Three months' hard labour for laughing at a policeman. On Saturday at Ennis, before Removables Hodder and O'Brien, two respectable young men, named Stephen J. Donleavy and William Brown were charged by District-Inspector Hill with having obstructed one Constable John Cole, in the discharge of his duty on the 1st inst. The obstruction, it was sworn, consisted in the defendants, while engaged in conversation, laughing at the constable. The pair of Removables sentenced the defendants to three months' imprisonment each to hard labour, in default of finding bail for their good behaviour. The defendants refused to give bail, and were then taken into custody."

In this case the prosecution was not under the Crimes Act at all. The young men deliberately walked up to the constable and insulted him, saying: "You are a scoundrel. You are the meanest man in Ennis, and we shall soon kick you out of Ennis." They were ordered to give bail, they refused and were imprisoned in default.

More outrageous still is the following example taken from *United Ireland* of March 9th, 1889:—"We think the consummation of the Coercion absurdity was reached at Fermoy Petty Sessions when Vigilant District-Inspector Ball prosecuted three young girls for calling sensitive Sergeant Doolan 'smiler,' and sapient Colonel Deane informed them that they might be sent to prison for twelve months for the diabolical crime."

The young girls in question were three women, one elderly, and were ringleaders of a crowd who mobbed the police, calling them "bloodhounds," "murderers," and using obscene expressions. On being brought before the Court, they expressed regret, and were let off with a caution.

The "Brave Little Girl" Fiction.

Here is a good example of the Nationalist lie, as circulated. Mr. Harrington, M.P., in his pamphlet called "A Diary of Coercion," on page 13 has a section headed "Imprisoning Children." In his note he says: "In this case a number of school-children groaned two men named Stephen Murphy and Daniel Murphy;" while Mr. Samuel Laing, in referring to the same case, talks of a certain Mary Anne Lawlor (mentioned by Mr. Harrington as a little girl), as "a little girl of fourteen who was sent to gaol for a fortnight for saying 'boo' to an emergency man." This story, circulated in thousands of copies through Great Britain, is only a specimen of shameless falsehood. Mary Anne Lawlor was no school-girl, but a determined woman who gave her own age as twenty-six! She assembled with some men outside the Murphys' house, where they shouted, yelled, and blew horns. Being a woman, the magistrates offered to let her off if she would promise not to annoy the Murphys again, but she refused.

We have given these only as *specimens.** To the same category of fiction belong the stories of the old women of seventy-five who have been imprisoned, and of the little boys vending newspapers. Most disgraceful of all is it, that detection never seems to kill the Home Rule lie. The false story of Mary Anne Lawlor is still circulated. The speaker who is confronted with these or similar tales, should insist on having chapter and verse given for each statement. Once he gets the alleged name and date, he will invariably be able to prove either that the entire story is false, or that it is based on a wholesale suppression of material facts. He may, also with effect, ask under what section of the Crimes Act is such a fiction possible? No worse feature of the Parnellite agitation is there than the fact that week after week fresh stories are invented, and copied eagerly by the Home Rule press of Great Britain.

THE REAL COERCION.

As to the Coercion practised by the Nationalist tyrants in Ireland, it is equally impossible to give instances at length. It is only possible to refer the speaker to those sources from whence he can procure reliable information and full particulars.

Two main forms of Coercion have been for the last nine or ten years practised on tenants in Ireland. These are—

1. Murder and outrage.
2. Boycotting.

* For further examples see "Some Pattern Fables Examined," being an Appendix to "The Truth about the Irish Question." Liberal Unionist Association.

It will at once be seen that within the limits of this work it would be quite impossible to give a full account of each crime. The following list may, however, prove useful:—

Murders and Attempts to Murder for Agrarian Objects.

Year.	Number.	Year.	Number.
1879	4	1885	8
1880	38	1886	12
1881 ...	32	1887	21
1882	63	1888	16
1883	25		
1884	9		228

As a recent illustration of the way in which the unwritten law is enforced, the following is valuable:—

OUTRAGES COMMITTED ON THE KENMARE ESTATE FROM NOVEMBER 1ST, 1888, TO JULY 31ST, 1889, IN FURTHERANCE OF THE PLAN OF CAMPAIGN.

Particulars.

November 19, 1888.—Cattle of Patrick Cronin driven off a farm which he was grazing, to compel him to join the Plan.

December 5.—Outhouse of Arthur O'Leary maliciously burned, because he had not joined the Plan. The cattle (11 head) were saved.

January 1, 1889.—House of Michael Cooper broken into, shots fired, windows broken, and Cooper's dog killed.

February 28.—Shots fired outside the house of Thomas Groves; a notice found in his field threatening him with the destruction of his cattle if he did not remove them.

March 3.—House of John O'Connor broken into by Moonlighters, who fired shots and beat him severely for not having removed his cattle.

March 17.—House of Humphrey Moynihan fired into and his horse shot because he had not removed his stock.

March 25.—Two notices found threatening to shoot T. P. Moynihan and J. M'Carthy for not having joined the Plan.

March 29.—Moonlighters visited John Mahony and John Horgan, and ordered them to remove their cattle. Before leaving they fired shots.

May 3.—Turf destroyed on John Mahony's farm because he did not join the Plan.

May 10.—A colt and donkey of Michael Cooper shot because Cooper persisted in not joining the Plan. The eye of the colt shattered, and the donkey injured in the head.

May 19.—Three shots fired at the cattle of Patrick Cahill and Michael Moynihan. Two of the cattle were injured with shot.

June 21.—House of Robert Sullivan visited by Moonlighters, who fired shots. The reason given was that he had not joined the Plan.

June 30.—Two cows of Florence Sullivan stabbed because he paid his rent on 25th. One of the cows died.

June 30.—Four cows of John Keane and one cow of Timothy Counihan stabbed because they had paid their rents. Counihan's cow died.

July 17.—Dwelling-house of Giles Cooper fired into because he had not joined the Plan. The men were detected in the act by the police, who secured two of the party.

Boycotting.

Boycotting has been the second method employed to coerce the tenantry of Ireland. The following list of offences for which this punishment has been applied is of interest :—

1. Caretaking.
2. Herding.
3. Being a landlord.
4. Acting as agent.
5. Associating with those already boycotted.
6. Supplying the police.
7. Accommodating obnoxious persons.
8. Not joining the League.
9. Being related to a boycotted person.

10. Giving evidence.
11. Driving the police.
12. Not voting for Nationalists.
13. Being appointed a National School teacher.
14. Being suspected of having paid rent.
15. Not paying rent to local trustees.
16. Having dared to obtain compensation for being shot at.

What is Boycotting?

So much misconception exists in Great Britain on the subject of boycotting, that it is right for the speaker to inform English and Scotch audiences of what boycotting actually is. It means—

1. Deprival of all social intercourse. No one will speak to you.
2. Ruin in your business. No one will buy what you have to sell.
3. Starvation. No one will give you the necessaries of life, even in return for money. You become dependent on the police.
4. Education denied to your children. The children of a boycotted man are often driven from school.
5. It may besides mean, and often does mean, refusal of coffins to the dead; and it certainly entails—
6. Mutilation of your cattle.

Boycotting not Exclusive Dealing.

That boycotting is *not* mere exclusive dealing is not only evident from the above, but has been asserted by Mr. Gladstone himself in the following words:—"Exclusive dealing is a totally different thing. That has nothing to do with combined intimidation exercised for the purpose of inflicting ruin, and driving men to do what they do not want to do. That is illegal, and that is the illegality recommended by the hon. gentleman" (Mr. Dillon).—Speech in the House of Commons, May 24th, 1882 (*Hansard*).

The Initiation of Boycotting.

Boycotting in Ireland, *as an institution*, is entirely due to Mr. Parnell. The following words embody his official direction to adopt it as a policy:—

"When a man takes a farm from which another has been evicted you must shun him on the roadside when you meet him, you must shun him in the streets and the town, you must shun him at the shop counter, in the fair, and in the market place, and even in the house of worship—leaving him severely alone. By putting him into a moral Coventry, by isolating him from the rest of his kind as if he were a leper of old, you must show him that that is your detestation of the crime he has committed."—*Ennis, Sept. 18th*, 1880.

Boycotting the Parnellite Policy in 1888.

"I want to tell you here to-day to mark the enemy and shun him. The word used to be in the old days agitate, agitate, agitate: the word in the present day is *boycott, boycott, boycott*."—*Mr. John O'Connor at Tipperary, Oct. 7th*, 1888.

Boycotting still the Parnellite Policy.

The concluding sentence of the above was repeated by the same member of Parliament (Mr. John O'Connor) at the meeting of the National League of Great Britain, held in Manchester on Saturday, Sept. 28th, 1889. It is important, in view of the fact that the Parnellites try to take the credit for themselves or for Mr. Gladstone of every improvement in the state of Ireland.

On July 9, 1889, Mr. Thomas Mayne, M.P. for Mid Tipperary, swore as follows:—

"I would carry boycotting to the extent of selling nothing to a man, not even the necessaries of life."—(*Special Commission.*)

A Home Ruler on Boycotting.

A well-known Irish Protestant Home Ruler, Mr. T. W. Rolleston, quarrelled in May, 1888 with the National League on the question of boycotting. He has written a sixteen-page pamphlet on the subject, the following extracts from which will be useful for quotation. It should be explained that Mr. Rolleston's paper was written in reply to one by Mr. Samuel Laing, formerly M.P. for the Orkney and Shetland Islands:—

"I have known a man ruthlessly boycotted by a whole country side, and his life attempted, *simply for taking a situation from which a drunken, dishonest bog-ranger was dismissed*, who used to take money from the neighbours to let their cattle break in upon his master's land. *The Coercion Act saved that man.* He stood to his post, prosecuted his enemies whenever he could. At last they got tired of it, and he is now, I believe, rather a popular person in the neighbourhood. I, or any man, would ten times rather have spent six months in Tullamore Gaol, with or without prison clothes, than in the state of persecution in which this man lived for longer than that time. And, measuring his relief against Mr. O'Brien's imprisonment, I am not prepared to call the Coercion Act a purely oppressive measure.

* * * * * * * *

"Mr. Laing argues as if boycotting simply meant the punishment (he again and again shirks all definition of the nature of the punishment) of persons who take farms from which others have been harshly evicted. *It has in reality become an engine for the wholesale suppression of independent thought, of honest enterprise, and industry; for the handicapping of sober, honest, hardworking men all over Ireland* down to the level of the drunkards and idlers, of those who would rather get twenty-five per cent. off their rent by clamour and intimidation than treble their profits by toil and thrift. The future of Ireland demands that this vice be cut away root and branch. It is folly to talk of restricting and guiding it: its introducers have never tried to do so, and who else can? Only with unqualified and universal condemnation can it ever be effectively met.

* * * * * * * *

"Now, boycotting in Ireland is never confined to 'moral' coercion; and no one would care a straw for it if it was. The refusal of social intercourse can always be lived down, and a man will endure it for a time for the sake of gain. The refusal of the necessaries of life, itself a kind of physical violence, is now little felt, unless, perhaps, mortal sickness comes in to assist the moral coercionists. There are societies for the combating of the latter, whose ramifications extend throughout all Ireland. Few boycotted persons need, I take it, be unsupplied with necessaries at the usual prices. It is deeply to the disgrace of the Irish gentry if there are any. But no boycotted person is safe without a police escort.

"*The fact is that, speaking broadly, boycotting is murder.*

* * * * * * * *

"And when Norah Fitzmaurice, on her return to Kerry, is fiercely boycotted, and two of her persecutors sent to gaol—miscreants proved to be guilty of something even baser than the murder itself—*a Parnellite member gets up in Parliament, with the tacit approval of his party, to protest against the severity of their sentence.*" (On April 24th, 1888.)

Mr. Gladstone on Boycotting.

"What is meant by boycotting? In the first place, it is combined intimidation. In the second place, it is combined intimidation made use of for the purpose of destroying the private liberties of choice, by fear of ruin and starvation. In the third place, that being what boycotting is in itself, we must look to this: that the creed of 'boycotting,' like every other creed, requires a sanction, and that this sanction of 'boycotting,' that which stands in the rear of boycotting, and by which alone 'boycotting' can be made effective—is the murder which is not to be denounced."—*Speech in the House of Commons, Aug. 24th,* 1882.

Report of Royal Commission upon Boycotting.

The foregoing will be effectively corroborated by the words of the Report of the Cowper Commission :—

"We deem it right to call attention to the terrible ordeal that a boycotted person has to undergo, which was by several witnesses graphically described during the progress of our inquiry. The existence of a boycotted person becomes a burden to him, as none in town or village are allowed—under a similar penalty to themselves—to supply him or his family with the necessaries of life. He is not allowed to dispose of the produce of his farm. Instances have been brought before us in which his attendance at Divine service was prohibited; in which his cattle have been, some killed, some barbarously mutilated; in which all his servants and labourers were obliged to leave him; in which the most ordinary necessaries of life, and even medical comforts, had to be procured from a long distance; in which no one would attend the funeral of, or dig a grave for, a member of a boycotted family: and in which his children have been forced to discontinue attendance at the National School of the district. Had we thought it necessary for the purpose of our inquiry, we could have taken a much larger amount of evidence to prove the existence of severe boycotting in very many districts. We did not, however, think it necessary to examine more than a sufficient number of witnesses to inform ourselves and to illustrate the cruel severity with which the decrees of local self-constituted tribunals are capable of being, and are actually, enforced."

Cases of Boycotting.

The speaker who desires these is recommended at all times to choose the latest possible cases. These he will find recorded each month in the *Liberal Unionist* newspaper, or in *Notes from Ireland* (a fortnightly publication of the Irish Loyal and Patriotic Union). Numerous instances are to be found of course in the evidence taken by the Cowper Commission.

Statistics of Boycotting.

The following figures, which may be compared with those on p. 152, show again that neither Mr. Gladstone nor the "union of hearts" has reduced crime and intimidation, but that the policy of the Crimes Act has.

During Mr. Gladstone's "Coercion."

From April to June, 1885, the number of persons wholly and partially boycotted was 299

Mr. Gladstone's Act Expired.

From July to December, 1885, the number was 891

and

On August 31st, 1887, the number had risen to 4,556

[From the time of Mr. Gladstone's conversion to Home Rule until Mr. Balfour's Act came to be applied in the autumn of 1887, boycotting increased more than fivefold.]

During Mr. Balfour's "Coercion."

On December 31st, 1887, the number had fallen to ... 2,469
On December 31st, 1888, to 712
On August 31st, 1889, to 313

The figures quoted are, of course, as all through this volume, taken from Parliamentary returns.

GLADSTONIAN SPEECHES ABOUT COERCION.

It is hardly necessary to say that the speeches of Sir George Trevelyan are a perfect mine for those who desire to seek for quotations in support of the Crimes Act, or against the Coercion of the League. The following extracts are samples :—

> "The party of order includes every farmer who does not want to rob the landlord of his due, and who does not want to be forced to pay blackmail to agitation—every poor fellow who desires to be at liberty to earn a day's wages, by whomsoever they are offered him, without being shunned, insulted, beaten, or too probably murdered." (Speech at Hawick, Feb. 10th, 1883.)

> "Why did Lord Spencer leave such a very hateful memory? I should imagine the reason was that he vindicated law and order." (Speech in House of Commons, April 8th, 1886.)

> "Nothing but the fact that the police and resident magistrates were in the hands of a strong central government preserved certain districts in the south-west of Ireland from wholesale massacre." (Speech at Selkirk, June 30th, 1886.)

> "What is called COERCION was merely the putting in force of the steps which are required to ensure conviction, and to carry out the ordinary law." (*ib.*)

Almost equally effective for the same purpose are the speeches delivered by Mr. Gladstone himself in the House of Commons in the Sessions of 1881–82, and set out in *Hansard's Parliamentary Debates.* Thus, speaking of the failure to administer justice in Ireland, Mr. Gladstone said :—

> "That breaking-down means the destruction of peace

and all that makes life worth having; it means the placing in abeyance of the most sacred duties and most cherished rights; it means the establishment of the servitude of good men, and the supremacy and impunity of bad men." (Jan. 28th, 1881.)

"By 'boycotting,' he" (Mr. Dillon) "means nothing but merely ruining men who claim to exercise their private judgment in opposition to his; that is all he means. What I say is this, that men who resort to illegality as a policy, a system, within certain limits, have no right to expect the observance of those limits *by others*." (May 24th, 1882.)

"The article of justice satisfies me perfectly; but I must remind the hon. member that it means justice to all and to every one. Unfortunately, this includes the use of force for the punishment of evildoers, and the praise of all who do well." (May 19th, 1882.)

"We shall not cease to press our proposals on the British Parliament, and we feel confident that we shall have a truly national assent and support to this assurance, that our effort is an honest effort to restore to Ireland the first condition of Christian and civilised existence." (Speech on introduction of Protection of Property Bill, Jan. 28th, 1881.)

Respect for the Law a Radical Doctrine.

With the above quotations we may well compare the following extract from a speech delivered by Mr. Chamberlain at Birmingham (Jan. 29th, 1887):—

"If a law is bad, let us strenuously endeavour to amend it; but as long as it exists, respect the law because it is the law, because it is the collective expression of society, the voice of the community for the protection of all its members. Respect for the law is the only thing which stands between us and that pernicious doctrine that might makes right, which it has been the boast and the glory of the democracy to supersede. What is the law? The law is the security of the weak against the strong; it is the protection of the poor against the rich; it is the safeguard of the few against the many. If you destroy the law, which is the highest expression of the democratic idea of equality, you will have to take your choice between anarchy on the one hand and despotism on the other; and, to my mind, it is a suicidal course for any Radical to lay sacrilegious hands on this great edifice of our freedom."

In conclusion, we may once more point out that the speaker should on all occasions make it clear that the question is one of the "Coercion" of the Law *versus* the Coercion of the Law-breakers.

Part IV.

SUPPLEMENTAL.

UNDER this heading we add a few paragraphs giving information on certain points which hardly fell within the three main divisions of this work.

THE PARNELLITES.

In view of the fact that a Special Commission is at present sitting to hear evidence about the antecedents and past doings of these gentlemen, silence on many matters is at present requisite. There are, however, some aspects of the matter well worthy attention.

Their Literature.

The chief weekly paper of the Parnellite Party is *United Ireland.* Of that journal Mr. Parnell is part proprietor and Mr. William O'Brien *editor.* The following are specimens of its attacks on English Liberal Ministers:—

> "He" (Lord Spencer) "stuck at nothing—not at secret torture; not at subsidising red-handed murderers; not at knighting jury packers; not at sheltering black official villainy with a coat of darkness." (June 13th, 1885.)
>
> "What is to be thought of the honour or decency of men like Earl Spencer and Mr. Trevelyan, who, knowing the atrocious crimes of which French has been guilty, not only keep him on in their service and allow him to draw his salary, but connive at his shamming to escape from justice?" (Aug. 3rd, 1884.)

> "In the art of wriggling, the eel and George Otto Trevelyan lick the whole animal kingdom." (Sept. 27th, 1884.)

> "Mr. Trevelyan continues to maintain his reputation as, upon the whole, the meanest, poorest, spitefullest creature who ever held sway in Ireland in the name of England." (Oct. 24th, 1885.)

Scores of similar quotations compounded of filthy abuse and lies without measure will be found in "*United Ireland* on *Spencer*, *Trevelyan*, *Gladstone*" (a pamphlet issued by the Irish Loyal and Patriotic Union).

The best condemnation of this wicked method of attack is to be found in Mr. W. O'Brien's own evidence tendered in the course of his action against the *Cork Constitution* in July, 1888:—

> "After reading an article in *United Ireland* comparing Lord Spencer to Strafford, Mr. Atkinson, Q.C., asked Mr. O'Brien—'Does not the article convey that Lord Spencer was guilty of killing innocent men?' *A.* 'It condemns the system.' *Q.* 'Does it not condemn Lord Spencer?' *A.* 'Unfortunately it does; somebody should be taken as the responsible person. Earl Spencer was the figure-head, and he had to be attacked.' Mr. O'Brien then explained that 'now they knew' Lord Spencer's real character, they regretted they had said a great many things that they now knew to be *scandalously false* as of himself, but most unquestionably true in every particular of that system of government for which he was responsible. However, if Lord Spencer were to bring an action against him for libel, he" (Mr. O'Brien) "would offer a very humble apology, and would put in a plea of justifiable criticism." (See *Times' verbatim* report, July 27th, 1888.)

The importance of passages like these lies in the fact that Englishmen and Scotchmen are now asked to believe *the same things of the present Government by the same men.* Are the convicted liars of 1882-85 to be trusted as truth-tellers now when they repeat the same old story?

But the Parnellites have also a daily paper in Ireland, the *Freeman's Journal.* From that organ the following extracts should prove useful:—

"We contend that the good government of Ireland by England is impossible, not so much by reason of natural obstacles, but because of the radical, essential difference in the public order of the two countries. This, considered in the abstract, makes a gulf profound, impassable—an obstacle no human ingenuity can remove or overcome.

"It is that the one people" (the Irish) "is Christian, and the other" (the English) "non-Christian; the one animated by a supernatural principle, the other by a natural. Now, the methods and aims of two such societies must radically differ. There is between the two orders an incompatibility, not only antagonistic, but destructive. They cannot freely co-exist in the same society. They may be present, but it must be, not as equals, but in subjection and domination; not in peace, but in conflict. . . .

"Let us, as stout old Johnson advises, 'clear our minds of cant,' and we will find ourselves bound by reason and logic to deny to English civilisation the glorious title of Christian, for it contradicts in its form and essence the first principles of Christianity. . . . To put the contrast again in the plainest form—the one order of civilisation is Christian, the other non-Christian; the one people" (the Irish) "has not only accepted but retained with inviolable constancy the Christian; the other" (the English) "has not only rejected it, but has been for three centuries the leader of the great apostacy, and is at this day the principal obstacle to the conversion of the world. . . .

"The Christian idea is absolute, and will brook nothing that is not itself." (*Freeman's Journal*, Feb. 18th, 1886.)

Their Speakers.

Chief among the men sent down to constituencies to delude the British public are such gentlemen as the following:—

1. MR. JOHN O'CONNOR, once a member of the Fenian body. Organised an insulting demonstration in 1885 against the Prince and Princess of Wales. Twice imprisoned on suspicion of treasonable practices by Mr. Gladstone. Declared in November, 1886, "that he had lately been using language in favour of moderation and conciliation to such an extent in England that he feared he would not know how to address a Land League Meeting." (*Freeman's Journal*, Nov. 22nd, 1886.)

2. MR. JOHN DILLON, once a medical student, but no more. Described by Mr. Gladstone as "the apostle of a creed which is a creed of force, which is a creed of oppression, which is a creed of the destruction of all liberty." (*Hansard*, May 24th, 1882.) Famous for his opinions on—

   (*a*) *Rent.* "I will show him men who can pay and won't pay, because I tell them not to pay." (*Freeman's Journal*, Jan. 24th, 1887.)

   (*b*) *Vengeance.* "Let that man be whom he may, his life will not be a happy one, either in Ireland or across the seas, and I say this with the intention of carrying out what I say." (*Freeman's Journal*, Aug. 24th, 1887.)

   "It is the duty of every man in this country who has an Irish heart in his breast, and who feels for his country, to do everything in his power to injure everybody who helps Hamilton" (a land-agent). (Speech at Arklow, *Freeman's Journal*, Dec. 3rd, 1887.)

   (*c*) *Treatment of Cattle.* "If the landlord should put cattle on them, the cattle won't prosper very much." (Speech at Kildare, Aug. 15th, 1880. *Official Report—Queen v. Parnell.*)

3. MR. T. D. SULLIVAN, ex-Lord Mayor of Dublin, from the impoverished ratepayers of which city he received £6,000; a poet who has written the following doggerel lines :—

"England fears for India,
  For there her cruel work
Was just as foul and hateful
  As any of the Turk.
But when God sends us thither,
  Her rule to overthrow,
With fearless hearts, rejoicing,
  To work His will we'll go.

Stupid little England
  Thinks to say us nay,
But paltry little England
  Shall never stop our way."

Mr. Sullivan has composed a eulogy on the murderers of a policeman.* He *still* prints, publishes, and sells these poems, and also a book which he and his brothers have compiled, called "Speeches from the Dock," in which Jeremiah O'Donovan Rossa and other scoundrels appear for admiration.

4. MR. WILLIAM O'BRIEN.—This gentleman's career as editor of *United Ireland* is well known. In that capacity he grossly libelled Lord Spencer and Sir George Trevelyan. Famous for his "breeches" and his "sandwiches." Went out to Canada in 1886 to insult Her Majesty's Viceroy. Put in prison on suspicion of treasonable practices by Mr. Gladstone.

5. MR. T. P. O'CONNOR, President of the Irish National League of Great Britain.

He and his colleagues issued the following manifesto to the Irish voters in Great Britain on Friday, November 20th, 1885. It had been submitted to Mr. Parnell, and by him approved and ordered to be circulated :—

* *See* Song, "God Save Ireland."

"High upon the gallows-tree
Swung the noble-hearted three"—

i.e., Allen, Larkin, and O'Brien, who murdered Sergeant Brett at Manchester.

"*To Our Countrymen in England and Scotland.*

"The Liberal Party are making an appeal to the confidence of the electors at the General Election of 1885, as at the Election of 1880, on false pretences. . . . We feel bound to advise our countrymen to place no confidence in the Liberal or Radical Party, and so far as in them lies to prevent the government of the Empire falling into the hands of a party so perfidious, treacherous, and incompetent. In no case ought an Irish Nationalist to give a vote, in our opinion, to a member of the Liberal or Radical Party, except in some few cases in which courageous fealty to the Irish cause in the last Parliament has given a guarantee that the candidate will not belong to the servile and cowardly and unprincipled herd that would break every pledge and violate every principle in obedience to the call of the Whip and the mandate of the Caucus. We earnestly advise our countrymen to vote against the men who coerced Ireland, deluged Egypt with blood, menace religious liberty in the school, the freedom of speech in Parliament, and promise to the country generally a repetition of the crimes and follies of the last Liberal Administration.

"(Signed) T. P. O'CONNOR, President of the Irish National League of Great Britain.

"Justin McCarthy, Thomas Sexton, T. M. Healy, J. E. Redmond, James O'Kelly, J. G. Biggar, Executive."

The above gentlemen are supposed to constitute the "stars" of the Irish Party on the platform.

LIST OF USEFUL BOOKS.

The following books are earnestly recommended :—

"England's Case against Home Rule." Professor Dicey.

"As It Was Said." Published by the Irish Loyal and Patriotic Union.

"History of the Legislative Union." T. Dunbar Ingram. LL.D. (Macmillan & Co.)

"Irish Legislative Systems." New Edition. Right Hon. J. T. Ball, LL.D. (Longmans, Green & Co.)

"The Truth about Home Rule." Edited by Sir G. Baden-Powell.

"The Truth about the Irish Question." By "An Irish Peasant." (Published by the Liberal Unionist Association.)

"The Irish Union, Before and After." A. K. Connell.

"Chez Paddy." ("Paddy at Home.") Baron Mandat Grancey.

"Ireland Under Coercion." W. H. Hurlbert.

"Disturbed Ireland." By T. W. Russell, M.P.

Together with all publications issued by the Liberal Unionist Association and the Irish Loyal and Patriotic Union.

CONCLUSION.

We have now completed this survey of the Irish Question. The student may well say, in the words of Mr. Gladstone, which were true when they were spoken at Aberdeen in 1871, but which Land Acts, Arrears Acts, Franchise Acts, Relief Acts, have made incomparably more true in 1889:—

"I have looked in vain for the setting forth of any practical scheme of policy which the Imperial Parliament is not equal to deal with, and which it refuses to deal with, and which is to be brought about by Home Rule. . . . There is nothing Ireland has asked, and which this country and this Parliament have refused. This Parliament has done for Ireland what it would have scrupled to do for England and for Scotland. . . .

What are the inequalities of England and Ireland? I declare that I know none, except that there are certain taxes still remaining which are levied over Englishmen and Scotchmen, and which are not levied over Irishmen; and, likewise, that there are certain purposes for which public money is freely and largely given in Ireland, and for which it is not given in England or Scotland."

END.

For Speaker's Notes.

www.ingramcontent.com/pod-product-compliance
Lightning Source LLC
Chambersburg PA
CBHW030838270326
41928CB00007B/1115

* 9 7 8 3 7 4 4 7 4 0 7 5 3 *